What people are saying about Internet Millionaire Jeff Usner

I am no longer afraid of what would happen if I lost my current job!
- Joe Willingham

The Reverse Online Profit System is content OVERLOAD! Jeff definitely under promised and over delivered on this one!
- Richard Dennis

This is awesome! Very practical methods of doing business online. Thanks you for all your energy and sharing what you know.
- Hong Tran

Jeff is and was amazing. My expectations were exceeded.
- Larry

Jeff, I didn't know you had such a great sense of humor! Thank you for giving us so much. I can't wait to grow my business with what I learned and impact the marketplace.
- Maria Newton

Jeff, you have shared such valuable information. I was stuck because I did not "know how"; now I can move forward.
- Jennifer Ledford

Jeff in an amazing leader and teacher. I see an actionable step to crush my local market as well as my traffic.
- Mike Raett

I couldn't have asked for more. Thank you for all the nugget's of info that have opened up or lifted the barriers I was facing.
- Jeanette Maldonado

It was an honor to be a part of this and have Jeff share all the in's and out's of how to make this work.
- David Cook

This is something I have struggled with for over 10 years. I have lost a lot of money and quit over and over. No one has ever shared this kind of information. There's a lot of garbage out there and it is so easy to get lost. Thank you for showing us the path and caring so much.
- Bridgett Jolly

It was more than I expected: great exposure and real hope offered.
- Don Bailey

It's amazing!
- Alane Pearce

I feel I went from a dummy to a PhD in online marketing and advertising. Thanks!
- ...

INTERNET
MILLIONAIRE
Your Blueprint To Succeed

Internet Millionaire: Your Blueprint to Succeed

ISBN: 978-0-692-01798-2
Printed in the United States of America

Dedication

You are my Creator. You gave me the ideas in this book.
Apart from You, I am nothing. I dedicate this book to You.
My Savior, My Strongtower. Thank You for guiding me in
all I do.

Acknowledgements

First, thank you Jesus Christ for saving me from the path I was walking down. Thank you for taking me from brokenness, destitution, and destruction to where I am today. Thank you for allowing me to do what I do.

Thank you Jennifer. You are the most incredible wife I could have ever dreamt of. I am overly blessed with you as my companion through this amazing journey of life. Thank you for going through all the pregnancies, and births, to give us the most amazing family in the world. Thank you for your support, for your belief in me when all else was falling apart. Thank you for your vision, honesty, patience and encouragement. I love you and am grateful that you are my wife.

To all my children, thank you for your patience while Daddy worked on this project. I am so thankful you are my children. Joshua you inspire me with your vision and ideas. Joel, I am blown away by your faith, wisdom and knowledge! James, I love you and miss you. You have helped give me mission and purpose in my life. I miss you. John, thank you for your enthusiasm and making me laugh. Joy, you've got Daddy's heart. I am so grateful to have a beautiful, amazing daughter in my life.

Hans and Dani Johnson – thank you for your continued leadership in our lives. Thank you for your faith, action and heart. We love you and your entire family. I am so grateful for both of you pouring into our lives and being such a critical part of our lives and our transformation, in every area of our lives. You are both amazing!

To my unbelievable team! You all rock! Thank you Phil for taking the reigns and allowing me to step out and lead our company in a new direction. I appreciate your leadership on our team. Thank you Leah for putting up with my 'shotgun' method of business ideas and craziness. You have done an amazing job adapting, learning and growing. Thank you! Thank you Michael for taking over all our traffic while I have been so buried with writing this book. You have done an amazing job and we are blessed to have you and your family building with us everyday. Thank you Kate for all your wonderful help with our family and our household. You have made done an incredible job with our children and keeping our household moving forward (and less crazy!) Thank you Dom, Chelsie, David and Matt! You rock! Can't wait to see all that will come in the future from all of your hard work. All of you inspire me in your persistence, tenacity, and the fact that you can keep up with all the crazy ideas we pursue! Thank you.

Thank you to my team overseas. You all always go the extra mile in excellence. I appreciate all your extra hours pushing this project, and all our projects, to the finish line! I can't wait to meet you someday.

To Brother Harry, you are an amazing man of God who I have learned so much from. Thank you for your heart to serve and be used by God. Thank you for your words of encouragement, wisdom and knowledge. Thank you for being such a great friend and example to all of us.

Mom and Dad, thank you for being patient with me, encouraging me, and believing in me in all I set out to do throughout my life. Thank you. I love you both.

My wonderful in-laws, Judy and Leland Sharrock, thank you for sticking with me through all our moves, businesses and everything in between. I hope this book will finally put an end to you asking me when I will get a job.

Brian McFadden thank you for your wisdom, counsel and encouragement. I appreciate every moment I get to learn from you.

Jennifer Ratchford, thank you for 'encouraging'...ok, forcing us to do the Internet Millionaire Bootcamp in 2010. Without you, none of this would be happening right now.

Helen Chang, thank you for your guidance and leadership with directing this book. I could not have done this without you. I appreciate your heart for people and serving them in the best way possible.

Lenny Allene, thank you for getting me started with writing this book. If you wouldn't have flown all the way to the States for the wedding, this book wouldn't be in print. Thank you for your leadership and initiative to lead me in the right direction and take action.

Bryan and Dianne Schwartz, thank you for being there during some of the most difficult moments of our lives. We love you and your family and appreciate all you have done in our lives. You are a true inspiration to our entire family. We love you.

Thank you to my team overseas. You always go the extra mile in excellence. I appreciate all your extra hours pushing this project to the finish line! I can't wait to meet you someday.

Thank you ABC and Zodiak Media for taking a chance on me to be a part of the most amazing TV show, Secret

Millionaire. Thank you Leslie Garner for your leadership, direction and wisdom. Momma bear you are the best!

Thank you, reader. I appreciate you taking a chance and picking up this book. I hope this book inspires, instructs and educates you on how to grow the most successful business you can possibly build. I am grateful for your time and determined to hold nothing back in this book!

Table of Contents

Foreword

I grew up on welfare in a violently abusive, drug-infested home. I was constantly exposed to physical, emotional, mental, verbal, and sexual abuse–which produced a young lady who made very poor choices. By 17, I was pregnant out of wedlock. At 21, I found myself homeless with $2.03 to my name and $35,000 in debt. Depressed and suicidal, I finally said enough was enough, and I started a business from the trunk of my car and a phone booth. Within two years, I was a millionaire at the age of 23.

Today, I am a multimillionaire, owner of five companies, bestselling author, international speaker, business coach, and a radio talk show host who has been featured on hundreds of TV, radio and print interviews like Oprah Winfrey, The View, Good Morning America, Fox & Friends, the season premiere episode of ABC's Secret Millionaire, The Wall Street Journal, Forbes, and many others. I am also married with five kids and four grandkids.

Never did I imagine that this level of success would be possible for someone like me. This is why I am passionate about helping others reach levels of success they can't even fathom. Friend, you never know when your life is about to make a turn for the better. You have something in your hands right now that could be the very road map that will change your entire life.

When Jeff first came to us, he was in a very similar situation to what I had been in: he had a lot debt, no income, and his life was a mess. He was no stranger to hardships, deep struggles and failure. I personally watched Jeff pick his life up, become teachable, apply new financial and business strategies and then take his knowledge above and beyond — by developing a system that has helped him make millions of dollars.

Whether you realize it or not, there are a lot of sleazy people in today's world. There is so much corruption and bad leadership, fueled by selfishness and greed. In my line of work, I unfortunately encounter some of the worst of them. Jeff is not one of them. Time always tells the truth about a person's motives. So does spending quality time both personally and professionally. Jeff is a one of a kind. My husband and I both are beyond impressed with him.

Jeff has blown our minds with how far he has come and how humble he has remained. He is a man of honesty, integrity and the highest ethical standards. I have watched a lot of people come and go. It is a very rare opportunity to encounter someone as successful as Jeff — with a high level of expertise — who actually has a heart for helping others. His motives are pure and that is the ONLY reason why I am writing this foreword.

Most successful people from the Internet world could care less about you, your family or your needs. All they care about is soaking you of your cash, so they can run and blow it on a big house, fast cars and fast women. Jeff is the only expert from the Internet world I know who truly wants to see you succeed online and enjoy the lifestyle that it will afford you.

I trust that with this same exact system that is in your hands right now — if you choose to follow it — you will have the opportunity to do what Jeff has done: make millions with an online business. This system is not a trial. It works and it will work for you.

Jeff's powerful knowledge in the niche of Internet marketing is going to help you grow your income and take your life to a place that you did not even know was possible. Listen to what Jeff is telling you. As you're reading this book, take notes and study this craft. Maybe someday you'll be the next Jeff Usner, making millions, doing business with integrity, and building something that affects people's lives for the better.

It's time that you get started now. Don't wait. Turn the page, and begin your journey to writing your next success story by applying the things that Jeff is about to reveal to you.

~ Dani Johnson, Texas
Danijohnson.com
May 2012

Introduction

Frankly, I am surprised. . . .

Not just surprised, but shocked. I'm surprised, shocked, and actually laughing, just a little bit.

About you.

Why?

Well, it's not exactly about "you"; it's about you holding this book in your hands.

You shouldn't have this book. You shouldn't be reading this book. Because I shouldn't have written this book.

It's crazy to think how my life was just a few years ago. I had just lost my son, James. I had a stroke and almost died. I was scared and stressed out of my mind. I didn't even know how I could put food on the table for my family.

On top of all that, my businesses were falling apart. I was working long, long hours without drawing a salary. I was drowning in debt. I was depressed, overwhelmed, scared, hopeless, tired.

And, that's just the beginning of the story.

You see, you shouldn't have this book in your hands right now. Because a few years ago, I couldn't have taught you how to make a thousand dollars, let alone millions.

But, boy, how life can change.

You might be where I was. Afraid . . . overworked and underpaid . . . overwhelmed. Drowning in debt. Without hope, without vision. Not knowing what I was going to do next.

Yet, I had a dream, a desire, a burning passion inside me to become successful in all areas of my life. In my finances. With my wife. With my children. With my friends. With my God.

In all of these areas, I had a desire to become the best I could be.

And I still had a desire to become a millionaire—to be free from financial bondage. Making money without having to work endless hours. But how? How, under my circumstances?

More importantly, in your circumstances, how can you do it?

In this book, you will learn how I mastered the Internet and went from failure after failure to success after success and millions and millions of dollars.

I Am Excited for You!

I'm excited you have this book in your hands. If you are serious about changing your life, if you want to grow a successful business on the Internet, and at the same time have balance in your life, if you want a true "Internet millionaire" lifestyle, this is the book for you.

The Internet is a powerful medium to grow and scale any business. It allows you the opportunity to literally carry your office on your back wherever you go. Take a look at my life, and you will learn what you are about to discover in this book.

Here's how my life changed.

I went from being in deep debt, with no life to . . .

. . . traveling all over the world. Becoming debt-free. Accumulating assets. Being a star on ABC's *Secret Millionaire*. I bought a home with all cash. I paid off another home, and now I'm in the process of buying more homes in the most luxurious places in the world. It seems like I've been on vacation more than at work. Why? Because I can live anywhere. I get to live the Internet Millionaire lifestyle.

As long as I have an Internet connection, I'm in business. It's that simple.

I can be on a beach in Nicaragua or traveling through India, Europe, Israel—anywhere—and as long as I have an Internet connection, I can build a huge company.

I'm not sharing any of this to impress you. In fact, most of my friends have no idea I am an Internet Millionaire (that is, until this book was released or they saw me on ABC's *Secret Millionaire*). I'm not trying to impress you, just attempting to impress upon you what truly is possible.

You will learn the exact system I use every day to create the lifestyle I have. You are about to discover how I've cracked the code to be successful on the Internet and in life. I'm going to share with you how I went from being more than $285,000 in debt and worrying about how I was going to put food on the table, to becoming debt-free and creating a multimillion-dollar business online in less than eighteen months.

In this book, I'm going to share my personal journey from failure to success. I'll open up and reveal all my thoughts, ideas, mistakes, failures, and successes. I'll also divulge how I got on season 2 of ABC's *Secret Millionaire*. I will show you how to get to where you want to be.

My goal in this book is to help you get from wherever you are right now to wherever you want to go. I'll get into the nuts and bolts of growing a successful company, where I'll share how my companies are able to focus on the best money-making activities to create the greatest results and profits. You will learn how to use this same system and be as much as 500 percent more productive in half the time.

Make Your Money Grow

I'll also show you how you can make your money grow from a little to a lot —whether it's one dollar or a million dollars.

You'll learn the system you can use to make your first dollar online, and how to scale that to $10, $100, $1,000, and up to millions. It's the same formula we use every day to help any type of business from newbie enterprises to large corporations.

I'm also going to teach you how we get millions of people to our websites, how we convert these visitors to money, and how you can do the same in whatever business you are in.

DISCLAIMER:

This book does not get too technical. I am about the least technical person I know. Seriously, I've never built a website. I don't know how to do much of anything technical. I have learned a few skills, but I leave most of the heavy lifting of online technology to others. Don't worry, I'll show you how you can do the same thing, regardless of your current skill set.

You can expect a complete system on how to build any business on the Internet. I'll share how you can find money-making niches, how you can cut 90 percent of your failures, how to buy traffic on the Internet for up to 50 percent less than your competitor, and how to eat your competitor's lunch!

I'll also show you how to position yourself as the go-to company/product/service/business in whatever industry you are in. You'll learn how to get the most-qualified people to your website and through your front doors in three easy steps. And, you'll learn how, at a click of a button, you can make up to $6,000 for just a few minutes of work.

Sharing My Expertise

I now own several businesses in different markets with different products. They all have become successful using the same strategies, techniques, and tips you will learn in this book.

I am humbled and grateful that you are taking the time to read this book. You are different than most people I see.

You have the potential to achieve your dreams.

You have the potential to be as successful as in your dreams. You can grow your business, your relationships, your faith, and your family to whatever level you want to. It's up to you to decide.

Sharing My Story

Let me tell you my story.

How does someone go from broke, stressed and nearly dead to becoming an Internet Millionaire just a few years later and being on ABC's *Secret Millionaire*? How does that happen? That's a story in itself.

A few years ago, I went through two life experiences that changed my life forever.

I lost my son, James, at birth, and I had a stroke and

almost died. These were eye-openers, forcing me to take a serious look at why I do what I do.

I was living a good life. We had moved to Colorado, one of our favorite places in the world. Our kids Joshua and Joel were happy. My wife, Jennifer, was pregnant with our third child—a third boy. We had a great marriage, great kids, and incredible friends. We had a nice house with a paid-off Porsche and a BMW in the garage. We had some money in the bank. Our software/marketing company was growing, with fifteen to twenty incredible employees all focused on a bright future, in a 5,000-square-foot office. Our clients were excited about our services and software, and Jennifer and I had a clear vision of where we wanted to go in life.

All *seemed* well. All *seemed* right on the outside. We had momentum, we were moving forward, and we were excited about the future.

But the reality was anything but that. I wasn't happy. I was living a life I thought I'd never live.

Here I was, struggling on the inside. Working endless hours away from home. I was missing out on my kids' childhoods. I wasn't spending quality time with my wife and, as a result, we didn't have the passionate, loving relationship I yearned for. I didn't have the Internet lifestyle of my dreams.

In addition, I was starting to pile up massive debt in our business. I had invested most of our money in this new company. On top of all that, our company wasn't delivering on what we had promised our thousands of clients.

I was stressed out and overburdened with carrying the huge overhead we had to meet each month. Financial worries were stacking up fast. Money and bills dominated my thoughts, poisoning my marriage, my relationship with my kids, and my faith.

From the outside looking in, all appeared fine. But the harsh reality was that I was hanging on by a thread, fighting to keep it all together. I was walking on a tightrope and one wrong move, one more challenge, or one more bad day could send me falling to my death. My chin was primed for a major uppercut to take me out. One more challenge and that would be it.

I was certain life couldn't get much worse.

And then it did.

Giving Birth to Silence

We went to the hospital, checked in, and did the pre-birthing routine we experienced twice before with our first two sons, Joshua and Joel. Routine-wise, it was normal. Normal because we were going to go through childbirth with James.

As the birth progressed, the contractions increased with intensity, and the moment of birth came closer. All day in labor, I encouraged my wife. I did my best to be strong. Our good friends were outside the room praying and encouraging us. The day continued on, and finally we got to the moment of birth, with my wife — stronger than I could ever be — pushing and pushing.

My wife going through the pain and anguish a woman experiences in birth. Pushing and pushing. I could see James's head. The moment getting more intense and emotional. The doctor rushing into the room. The nurses overcrowding the tiny delivery room. My wife believing she would hear a cry when James when born.

We believed, and couldn't wait to hear the cry.

Finally, the moment arrived. James worked his way down the birth canal. It was the most intense part of the birth. James's head was almost out. He was about to come into our world. Pushing, pushing, one last push. The doctor pulled James up on my wife's stomach.

No cry. Just silence. Weeping. Tears. Horror. Exhaustion.

James was born. I cut the umbilical cord as many new fathers do. I cut the cord that had given James life. James weighed around 6 pounds.

My wife held him close. Looking into his eyes. Holding his hands. Looking at his cute little feet. Tears streaming down our faces. Looking at him. Our son. No life. No breath. Little arms, legs, head, nose — a baby boy. A gift from God. My hero.

We both held him closely for hours. Wrapped up in a newborn blanket. Smelling his head. Kissing his forehead. Sorrow. Not wanting to let go. Not wanting to accept what had just happened. Still believing in life. In shock.

My son was born.

I had just witnessed the strongest display of courage in a person I have ever seen. My wife: incredible, inspiring. I still don't know how I could ever have done what she did that day. Her actions still inspire me. She is an amazing woman.

James Amos Usner was born on August 15, 2007. We love him and miss him.

My life had been rocked. Could it get any worse?

As we struggled through the months after James's death, the workload continued to increase and the pressure mounted. I was working longer and longer hours, yet the debt continued to increase and my stress escalated. I just didn't think it could get much worse.

Every day I was coming home from the office feeling like a failure. I had stopped taking a salary from our company for months. And I was using our own personal finances to help the business stay alive.

On top of all of this, we endured two miscarriages after losing James. Stress continued building at home. Fear began to take over every area of my life. Fear of disaster. Fear of losing more children. Fear of losing our marriage. Fear of losing our businesses. Fear of losing our home. Fear of the worst.

My Health Scare

In December 2007, just a few months after losing James, I was at the gym doing my morning workout. Warming up by doing a light set on a weight machine, I pulled the bar down toward my head and suddenly felt a piercing, mind-blowing pain stab my skull. It felt like the right part of my head had exploded.

I felt ill and dizzy. I thought I must have blown a blood vessel. But I knew it wasn't from strain since these were light weights.

When I got home, I was still woozy, dry heaving at times, and had massive pain in my head. Jennifer told me to go to the doctor.

The doctor did a quick review and then sent me for a CAT scan. As I was lying on the CAT scan machine with the heat of the injected fluid running through my veins, thoughts continued to race through my head. What just happened? Am I going to be ok?

I finished the test and headed to my office a few blocks away. It wasn't long before the doctor called and said I needed to return to ER.

"What's wrong?" I asked.

A Stroke at 34

"You've had a stroke and we need you back here right away," the doctor replied. "We need to run more tests. You have some blockage in some arteries in your head, and there appears to be some major trauma caused by a stroke."

"What? I'm only thirty-four. I eat healthy. I exercise. Are you sure?"

"Yes, get to the ER now and call your wife. You've had a stroke and you are in serious danger."

In shock, my hands shaking, I hung up the phone, which felt like a 50-pound dumbbell. Thoughts racing through my head.

How could this be?

What do I tell Jennifer?

What is going on?

What if I die?

My kids, my wife, what will happen to them?

I wondered what to do. I was scared, confused, worried, petrified.

I took a moment to compose myself. Then I sank down in my office chair, tears streaming down my face. My face blank, staring ahead. A look of death dominating my face. Absolute terror, disbelief.

I can't believe this. How?

Why? What?

I couldn't believe what I had heard on the phone. I was in disbelief. Shocked.

I called my wife and asked her to come to the ER right away. I did my best to sound strong. To not sound afraid. But I don't think I did a good job of it. I was terrified, and she knew it.

Before I left my office, I told two friends what I had just

learned. I asked them to pray for me. I had heard of people being healed through prayer, so I told them to pray for a miracle or a healing.

Something.

I Don't Want to Die

At this point I thought, *I'll try anything. I don't want to die.*

As I made my way to my car, I thought about what the doctor had said. He believed I could have another "big" one at any time. A stroke that very day could end it all. I might not live to see tomorrow, to see my wife and kids.

All the stress over the business, the clients, work — suddenly none of it mattered. My mind was filled with my beautiful wife, whom I was so blessed to marry. And my boys: holding them, laughing with them. Watching them grow up.

God, please get me through this. Let me live.

As I drove to the hospital, I stopped at a red light. As I waited for it to change, fear, doubt, and worry continued pounding my head. Then, just as the light was about to change to green, I had the strangest feeling. I felt a kind of heat start at the top of my head and continue down my entire body.

My immediate reaction was, *Holy crap, I was just healed.*

I still don't know what happened. All I know is I felt different in that moment.

I walked into the hospital — the same hospital where we had spent some of the worst days of our lives during James's birth. And here I was again, another tragedy shattering our lives.

The familiar cold floors, blank walls, the hospital smell penetrating all of my senses. Everyone busy, looking at charts, doctors and nurses shuffling from one patient to the next.

I was ushered into an ER room, and a nurse handed me a gown and closed the curtain. Here I was. Behind a curtain. Same hospital. My head still spinning from the news I received. My mind racing with thoughts of worry, doubt, fear. As I put on the gown, my body was shaking. *What was going on?*

Within minutes, my wife arrived. We didn't exchange many words. She was in more shock than I was, so we just sat there. Waiting. Waiting for what was to come. Unsure of what was happening. Lost in the moment. This hospital was not friendly ground to our family.

Difficult Memories

Sitting in the ER with an IV in my arm, my wife at my side, I began to cry. Memories of James's birth came rushing back. The trauma and horror of that experience was fresh in my mind, and now the roles were reversed. Instead of my wife, I was the one in the hospital bed. The IV was in my arm. The gown was on me. The doctors were working on me.

Emotions overwhelmed me.

Was there any hope left?

How could things get worse?

There are moments in each of our lives when we question everything. Everything we believe in. Everything we've been taught. Everything we've seen or heard.

This was that moment for me.

After what seemed like hours of waiting, the doctor finally pulled the curtain aside. Within minutes I was whisked away for more MRIs on my brain, the first of many series of tests I would have that day and through the night.

They kept me in the hospital overnight—a long night by myself staring at a clock. Before my wife had left that evening, she had spoken with the doctor who said, "Be prepared for your husband not making it. Strokes usually happen together, and he could have another any time take his life."

So there I was, wondering what was going to happen. What was going on? Waiting to hear. Anticipating the worst news but, as with James's death, still believing this was just all a nightmare, and soon I'd wake up.

Questioning Everything

Lying in bed that night, unsure of the future, I began to question everything in my life.

I started to reflect very hard on why I was doing what I was doing. I began to form a new vision of what I wanted my life to look like. I asked myself questions like:

Why am I doing what I'm doing? How can I get rid of this stress in my life? What else can I do? What will happen if I die? My wife, my kids? What legacy am I leaving behind? Is there hope for me? Can I get my life where I want it? What do I want my life to look like? What do I want my marriage to be? What do I want my days to look like? Why am I stuck in this mess – again?

I was asking basic questions to discover what was most important to me. Why I was doing what I was doing.

I began to ponder and seek answers:

Who am I impacting? Why am I stuck here? And, more importantly, how do I get out? What is my new vision going to be? What matters most? How will my priorities be different? Where do I want to be 5, 10, or 20 years from now?

The clock seemed to tick-tock by very slowly. The hands

on the clock barely moving. Hour after hour, giving me time to examine my life. Examine and question everything.

Morning finally arrived. I asked the doctor about my situation.

"We can't explain it, but it appears all the damage is gone. There is no sign of stroke," she said. "All the trauma on your brain is gone. All the blocked arteries are clear. You are 100 percent healthy."

It was a true second shot at life. A second chance to do more, to be more, and to hope for more.

I walked away from the stroke alive. But I was still scared of my circumstances and unclear about how I'd change them.

As you begin this book, ask yourself why you are doing what you are doing. Why do you want your business to grow? What type of lifestyle do you want?

For me, I decided I would redesign my life. I would design my business around my lifestyle. You have to get clear about why you want your business to grow. Why do you want to start a business? Why do you want to take your business to a new level? If you are not a millionaire and you want to become one, ask yourself why.

Dig deep. The answers can't just be more money. It's got to go deeper.

I'm excited to walk this journey with you, and pray this book will help you make more money in your business, give you more freedom to do what you want to do, give you all the details you will need to succeed online, and just help you have more fun in your business and life!

Let's get started.

CHAPTER 1
Keys To Domination

Winning Basics

Michael Jordan is the best basketball player in the world. When he played, he was amazing to watch. He literally looked like he could fly effortlessly through the air. He'd dribble the ball down the court and take off from the foul line, while landing with a thunderous, rousing dunk to get the crowd cheering as if in ancient gladiator times.

Michael led his team to many championships, won dunk contest after dunk contest, won scoring title after scoring title, MVP after MVP. He also played on two Olympic gold medal-winning teams. He was simply the best to ever play the game. If you were playing against Michael, fear and the idea of losing would dominate your mind. When he set foot on the court it was "game over." Even when he was deathly sick in 1997 with a horrible flu, no sleep, and major dehydration, he almost single-handedly took the Utah Jazz out of the NBA playoffs.

He was simply amazing. We often remember his spectacular dunks and amazing grace on the court while flying to the rim. Yet, Michael invested most of his time in mastering the basics. He focused on becoming one of the best ever at dribbling, passing, and shooting. This is why he was so good.

There are many people who can dunk a basketball and fly through the air, but not many who can focus and master the basics. This is where the amateurs are separated from the professionals. Michael, who took major action, once stated, "I've missed more than 9,000 shots in my career. I've lost almost 300 games. Twenty-six times I've been trusted to take the game-winning shot and missed. I've failed over and over and over again in my life. And that is why I succeed."

Michael mastered the basics, took massive action, and became the best ever.

Master the Basics

I remember reading Michael Jordan's story and wondering how I could apply this to my life. I was never going to play in the NBA, but what could I learn from him and apply to business? I decided to master some basics, and it made all the difference on my way to becoming an Internet Millionaire.

I looked at myself and saw that I was good at a lot of things. I knew a little about a lot, but I didn't know a lot about just one subject. I hadn't mastered anything. When I changed this, my life changed forever.

I decided to learn everything I could learn about Internet traffic. In the Internet world, traffic is the measure of people visiting your website. When I started to look at how to master this, I realized there were many ways to get people to your website in the late 1990s and early 2000s. Some of those methods now are outdated.

Today, if I want to get people to my websites, I can write articles, learn organic search-engine optimization (SEO) marketing, post on forums, start a Facebook group, create Facebook fan pages, place Facebook ads, place an ad on Google, Yahoo, Bing or any search engine, build affiliate relationships, create videos on YouTube, master email marketing, buy media and banner ads, pin pictures on Pinterest, and the list goes on and on.

I had to make a decision. There were a lot of ways to get people to my website. I decided to master Google. I became laser-targeted on generating clicks from Google and converting those clicks to leads/people who would buy my products and services.

Hear me on this. We are going to talk a lot about dominating your market. One of the best ways to dominate a market is to become the one who decides to master the market. For me, that meant I did everything and anything on Google. I learned how to create ads that would crush my competitors. I discovered how to get my clicks for up to 70 percent less money than my closest competitors. I learned how to get millions and millions of keywords on Google so I could spank anyone who wanted to compete in my industry.

I literally owned the front page of Google search results for countless keywords. This means if you searched for "divorce lawyer," for example, you would see my websites on nearly every listing on the results page.

Why? Because I got singularly focused and mastered Google. You must treat this book seriously. If you master some of these basics, you will be successful with whatever business you do in life.

Let's dive into some fundamentals that, if you master, will elevate you to the top of any market, industry, or niche in business. You will become the "go-to" authority for whatever it is you do. You can become the Michael Jordan of your industry, while your competition shakes in their boots in fear of you.

It all starts with the basics. In this chapter, you are going to learn about basics in three areas:

- Millionaire Business Concepts

- Millionaire Marketing Basics

- Reverse Online Profits™ System

Millionaire Business Concept #1

Internet success is not about greed, power, and lust (as you might have heard from other books and events on Internet marketing) but about giving yourself and your business major leverage.

Leverage is one thing you must learn. Leverage allows you to make money through other people's efforts. Leverage makes the work of one have the power of the work of twenty to a hundred people. You must learn how to leverage yourself, or all you will do is what you can do yourself. And when it's just up to you, you limit the possibilities of your success and growth. Throughout this book, you will learn skills and secrets to leveraging yourself in several areas:

- Advertising

- Websites

- People

- Autoresponder emails

- Automation

Leverage gives you the ability to grow by hundreds of percentage points every year. Every second of every day, I have advertising, automation, websites, people, and systems working for me—whether I am at my kid's baseball game or sleeping in the middle of the night. Leverage is key.

Leverage is what has given me so much time and financial freedom. Without leverage through other people, advertising, and other technology, I could never be able to live the Internet lifestyle.

Leverage allows me to not be working, yet still making money. My business is not dependent on me. My businesses run on systems focused on leverage for maximum output with minimum efforts.

Millionaire Business Concept #2

Think laterally. Taking ideas from one industry into another industry is possibly the easiest way to get the extra push you need to take your business to the next level. Become a student of marketing. When commercials or infomercials come on TV, study them. When you see an ad on Facebook, click on it and ask why it is working or not working. The ad doesn't have to be in your industry. You may get a golden nugget from a Mercedes commercial and use it to double the profits in your business.

If you see an email from a company that gets your attention, ask yourself why. And then ask yourself, how could I use this in my business? I remember watching a commercial for a $100,000 Mercedes Benz and the main selling point was safety. I literally turned to my wife and said, "Honey, I'm sorry we don't have a Mercedes. I must not be a good dad." Why? Because this was the concept Mercedes was drilling into my head with its advertisement.

Could my family be safe in a 1980 Volkswagen Bug? Probably. I grew up hanging out in the back of a Plymouth station wagon with no seat belt or air bags, and I'm still here!

The point is to study what an advertiser is doing. When you go to McDonald's, the one question you always get is, "Do you want fries with that?" This one question increased many stores' profits by up to 39 percent! So ask yourself, how could I apply this in my business?

Copy What Works

The funny thing is there are many business owners who think they can conquer the Internet and be a millionaire by being original. You might have tried that yourself, but where did that take you? You don't have to be original to start. Just look at what is working right now, improve upon it, and launch it (as long as it is not infringing on copyright laws).

On the Internet, you can be original for two seconds; then your competitors, who have been online since the pre-historic period, will copy you and crush you on your own turf.

If something is successful in one industry, there is no reason why it will not bring you success in yours. There is plenty of inspiration. You can use ideas from one industry in another, ideas from one Internet traffic source in another, and simply apply what works in your endeavor to duplicate those successes.

Why do you want to do this? Because it saves time, effort, money, and headache. You will succeed faster, make more money, and have more free time and fun when you master this concept.

Millionaire Business Concept #3

What do you think is the No. 1 reason for failure in business, marriage, parenting, or health?

I believe it is the lack of focus.

Again, I repeat—businesses, marriages, and other endeavors fail when people lack focus.

Focus is something you must train yourself to do. You must develop this skill set and live it, breathe it, do it every day of your life. It's the difference between making it and breaking it. It's the difference between making your first dollar and not making your first dollar. It's the difference between making your first million and falling far short of your financial goals.

There is a lot going on around you all the time with numerous devices demanding your attention, and marketers and other people trying to turn your focus to their agenda. People push their products and services, as cell phones ring and emails stream in.

There are hundreds or thousands of potential distractions waiting to get you off course every day, to suck up your time, and bring your attention to where it shouldn't be.

Do you ever feel overwhelmed? Do ever feel like it's hard to focus? Do you ever get to the end of a day and sit back and wonder, "What did I do today? What did I accomplish?" Does this happen most days?

Too Many Distractions

Why is it so hard to have a productive day?

Focus is the No. 1 struggle for most companies, employees, business owners, parents, and grandparents. Focus is the No. 1 struggle for almost everyone.

But this is especially the case in the workplace. Whether you are an employee or you have your own business, here is what the typical person's day is like:

Most people work on or around a computer and a cell phone, checking or receiving the following:

- Facebook status updates (not business related)

- Text messages

- Instant messaging

- Twitter feeds

- Other websites

- Phone calls

Stop and think about how many times you check Facebook, email, text messages, Twitter, and voice mail in an hour. Or see an advertisement. I have heard that every distraction you encounter can cost you up to twenty minutes to get back on track to what you were doing. That's nearly a half-hour of lost productivity that you can't regain. In fact, a 2007 study by Basex estimated that distractions cost U.S. businesses $588 billion per year, and this high cost is likely repeated in organizations around the world.

In an eight-hour workday, if you average three distractions an hour that means most of your day is shot, worthless, devoid of results.

Many of you run a business apart from your regular job that you dedicate three or four hours to daily. If you have two distractions an hour during your work, your business will not grow. It will fail, and you will not be successful or make money. You might sink deeper and deeper into debt.

Distractions are the main reason most people fail in business.

Dismiss the Distractions

When I learned what I'm about to share with you, my businesses exploded. I often hear Phil, our chief operating officer, telling me, "I can't believe how much we get done in our office. It blows me away!"

It's because of focus. Focus is so critical. It's everything. How you spend your time, who you work with, where you work, and how you work all affect your focus.

If you have your own business, there may be clients you need to stop focusing on, because they are killing your time. Can you think of a client right now who seems to take up more time than all the others combined?

Now that you have the person in your mind, here's what I want you to do: fire him. Seriously. Fire him or her. Today. Don't wait. I don't care if that client makes up over half of your revenue. Fire the person or get someone else in your company to baby-sit him.

I've done this in our business even when it seemed insane. I've heard in the past, "Jeff, you are crazy. We can't afford to fire them." And I've done it, and it has turned out to be the best thing for our business.

Employers, listen up. You just heard me talking about firing clients.

Now, it's your turn. Who is the one employee who seems to waste the most time and cause the most distractions in your life and office?

What are his or her results?

So here's what you need to do: fire that person today. Hear me on this. This is critical. Don't think it will get better. Clients and employees who are distractions cost you a lot more money than if they did not work with or for you.

Some of you have more than one. Fire them all.

A Thirty-Day Pledge

Now that I've addressed employers and business owners, let me talk to the rest of you.

You are not getting off this exercise that easy. Here's what you need to do. (This goes for employers and business owners as well — you get double the work.)

I want you to look at your personal life and ask yourself what your biggest distraction is. Is it Facebook, your cell phone, texting, email, surfing the web, watching TV, or listening to a radio show? Once you identify the activity, you are going to stop doing it right now. Seriously.

For most of you, it's Facebook, so I am challenging you right now: Give up personal use of Facebook for thirty days. Give up watching for your friends' pictures and comments. Give up posting to your personal Facebook page. Your life will not look the same. Stop wasting time on this website and invest that time into your spouse, your kids, your business, your job, and your skill sets.

Communicate with people. Add a post that says: "I've decided not to log onto Facebook for the next thirty days. No, I'm not crazy. I just want to do a test to see how my life will be affected."

That's it. On Facebook, there generally are not any emergencies you need to tend to. If something is wrong, people usually don't just use Facebook to communicate the problem. If they do in your case, add this at the end of the statement: "If there is an emergency during these thirty days and you need to contact me, you can do so by _____." Provide another way to contact you, such as email or a text message.

But that's it. Do it!

Change Your Habits

Regarding email, you might be thinking, "Jeff, I can't give up email." Okay, you may not be able to give it up, but here is what you will do if you are serious about growing your business, expanding your income, getting promoted in your job, and making more money.

Form a new habit with email:

- Do not keep your email inbox open all day long on your computer.

- Only check email two or three times a day.

- Let your friends, family and/or employees know you are doing this.

- If there is something truly urgent, create a method to contact you.

- Be sure to define what constitutes an urgent situation. In this case, let the person know how to contact you (other than via email).

- Let people know you will only be checking email at 9 a.m., 1 p.m., and 4 p.m., for example, so they can better know how to communicate with you. If you are an employee, talk to your boss to see if this is okay for the workplace.

Remember, you're doing this to have fewer distractions, to stay focused, and be more productive. By the way, don't just stop replying to emails; the key to this exercise is communication, not neglect.

Next step: Turn off any instant messaging on your computer. (Again, you need to discuss this action with your boss if you use IM in the workplace.) If you are able to turn it off completely, do it. Ninety-nine percent of you who run your own business need to do this. Since many of you will think you are the 1 percent who doesn't have to turn it off, I'll revise my number to say 100 percent of you need to do turn off instant messaging and follow the six steps listed above about email.

A few years ago, I heard a story about Charles Schwab that changed my life forever.

Over 100 years ago, Charles Schwab was the President at Bethlehem Steel. He hired Ivy Lee to come into his company to consult and help Bethlehem Steel become more efficient, increase profits and operate at a higher level.

Ivy Lee told Charles Schwab he could help the company if he could meet with each of the executives for just 15 minutes each.

Schwab asked Lee, "How much will it cost me?"

Lee replied, "Nothing, unless it works. You can send me a check in 3 months for whatever you think it's worth."

Schwab hired Lee and brought him to meet with the executives. Lee only took about 10 minutes with each executive and said to Schwab after a short time, "Done".

He told Schwab what to have the executives do. And said, send me a check in 3 months.

Well, 3 months later Lee received a check for $25,000.00.

That was $25,000.00 over a hundred years ago, that's easily several million dollars today. So this one strategy Schwab gladly paid millions for.

Are you ready for this?

I can tell you since implementing this myself and with my team, my team and I have become the most focused group you can imagine. As Phil says, "I can't believe how much our team does. How much we get done is amazing."

Here's why – and I can say I would pay millions for this

idea as it has made me millions.

Ivy told Schwab, each day before the executives go home, have them create a top 6 list of the most important items they must accomplish the next day.

And, don't go on to the next task until you are able to cross out the previous task. This means – don't do anything the next day when you get to work or you sit down in your home office – don't do anything else but #1 on the list.

Then, when #1 is complete, cross it out and go on to #2, then once #2 is done move on to #3.

That's it.

Don't let the simplicity of this fool you. Simple is why it works. It works better than any time management book, course, tool I've ever used.

It works. Be sure to invest some serious thought into what are your top priorities. The best way to figure this out is to simply ask yourself, what is it in my day that brings the biggest results?

What do I do to make the biggest difference?

Take time now and do this: figure this out. Once you know what is most important and you do it, your business will explode.

But, you must follow this 100%.

This means you can't be in the middle of #1 and the phone rings and you answer it. Or your email makes a noise, and you must check to see what or who it is. Or your instant messaging beeps or pops up and you must know what and who it is.

These things should be off – as I've already discussed.

We are talking about pure 100% focus.

Did you know it's said the top CEO's in the world only get about 2-3 hours of really productive time a day? That's it. And they run multi billion dollar companies.

So if you are just starting out and you don't master this, how much of a chance do you have to succeed? I believe almost no chance. Let's move on to the next important basics you need to master.

Master Three Millionaire Marketing Fundamentals

Millionaire Marketing Fundamental #1

Sell what people want to buy. Find a hungry market and create a product or service they want to buy.

This is a marketing fundamental that most people seem to forget. What typically happens is we come up with ideas we think will work. We get excited about an idea. We share it with our friends (who usually know nothing about marketing). We share it with family; we write it down on paper. The idea becomes our little baby.

The problem is that until we put the idea into action, we don't know if it's going to work. In fact, if it's an original idea and no one else is doing it, it's almost bound to fail. It's much easier to go find something that is already working and do it better or in your own way and offer that to the market, versus coming up with new ideas and taking them to market.

Most new ideas fail. I don't want to discourage new ideas. There are always exceptions to the rule, but go find a hungry market first. Offer them a product or service they are already buying. Make a lot of money doing this. Then, start with your own ideas!

Years ago, I was overweight. I applied a system and lost about forty pounds in just over two months.

I loved the diet. I loved the idea of the diet. It worked. It still does. So I decided I would sell a book about this diet. But instead of looking at what the market was already buying, instead of looking at what books were already available, I decided to simply invest months of my time writing my own book. I invested a lot of money. I finally launched the book and no one bought it. Why? I didn't study the market enough to see exactly what people were buying. I was in a good market, but I didn't look at exactly what the market was buying at that point.

People were more focused on quick-fix pills (still are, to some extent) and not a program promoting weight loss through actual exercise and a proper diet. This trend has changed, and now people are more real about what it takes to lose weight. Just turn on the TV and see the infomercial selling the P-90X or Insanity workout program. That's about as real as it gets. But when I launched my book, people weren't buying programs in which they had to actually work to lose weight.

I wasted a lot of time and money. Don't make this mistake.

I realize markets change. People change. And there are a few exceptions to this rule. But for 99 percent of people just getting started and for 99 percent of established companies generating millions, the concept holds true. If you are the first with an idea, it's probably going to fail.

Find a product/service/opportunity people are already buying—a market where they are hungry and eager to spend money. Then, do the market research to create an offer they will buy. This is so easy. When you follow this marketing fundamental, success is almost guaranteed!

Millionaire Marketing Fundamental #2

Find where your market is and get in front of those potential customers.

This may sound simplistic, but I am always amazed at the answers I get from successful business owners when asked about how they think they can best get more clients. The answers usually never make any sense.

In this book, we are going to be talking a lot about traffic. This has to do with finding people who want to buy what you have to offer. There are countless ways to drive traffic to a website, but the easiest way is to simply find where your market is already going and simply "stand" in front of those customers with your offer.

One of the best ways to do this is to find out the source your market is already buying from and simply create a relationship with that company to offer your products. This can be a large company or small company. It doesn't matter. What matters is that the company you work with is already working with your potential clients.

This is called Joint Venture Marketing or host relationship marketing. When you are on the Internet, Joint Venture Marketing goes by the name "affiliate marketing." It's the same thing; one is done online and the other offline.

One of the first places I applied this marketing concept resulted in a huge success. I had started a company called Leadstore.com in early 2001, which did OK for years. We were able to help many businesses, but our growth didn't really explode until I applied this concept.

Here's how I did it. I found someone in that market who was already in front of my potential buyers. I created a relationship with them so I could present my products/services to their clients.

Within our first sixty days of applying this principle, our

company grew by 500 percent. A 500 percent growth in sixty days is amazing! The great thing is it's "no-risk" marketing. I'm not buying or spending a lot of money to get traffic to my website. I get the traffic for free. If the traffic converts to dollars, then I may pay out a commission for those sales. But, the key is there is no risk to me, as I am not the one sending the traffic (people) to my website. Someone else does this at their expense.

As mentioned earlier, when you set up these types of relationships online, it's often called "affiliate marketing." This is simply when you promote someone else's product/ service/company and you are paid a commission on the sale. (Sometimes it's per click or lead, but in most cases it's by the sale).

Major companies like Walmart, Dell, EBay, GoDaddy, Amazon, and others use this strategy to grow their businesses online.

You can also apply this strategy when you buy advertising.

I used this concept a few years ago to make my first $7,000 per day promoting someone else's weight-loss product.

In the month of December, I started to look ahead at what markets well in January. One of the most obvious markets I saw was weight loss. I also knew that Oprah always does a show in early January with millions of followers who want to lose weight.

The ideal concept here would have been going on Oprah's show. Well, that wasn't going to happen for me then. But what I could do was get in front of her followers by simply going to where they would go to find Oprah's website.

So, I went to Google.com and was able to rank as the

No. 1 result for Oprah.com so that when a person typed in Oprah.com on Google, my website ranked first. I'll teach you exactly how I did this in Chapter 5 and also show how you can use search engines to get an avalanche of traffic.

The day that episode aired, my website went crazy! I had a ton of people coming to my website, because they were all looking to lose weight. So my website was all about losing weight.

I found where my market (people looking to lose weight) was going. Then, I simply stood in front of the traffic with a sign saying "come to my website." And, they came.

Millionaire Marketing Fundamental #3

Be congruent in your marketing. Once you find what your market wants, what they respond to, and what they act on, then this message must be the message you use throughout your marketing.

Whether you are placing a banner ad on a website, an ad on Google, an ad on Facebook, sending an email, talking to someone on the street, writing a book, doing a radio or TV interview, or talking anywhere about your company, product, or service, you must use the same message.

This is one of the most common mistakes I see in marketing. Many people make money with something and never really understand why they made money. What was the compelling reason for someone to hand money over to you? What did you say? What did the ad say? What happened? Always look at your numbers. Always know where success is coming from and where failure is coming from. Then, simply turn off the losers and crank up the winners.

That's marketing 101.

Let's go through an example of non-congruency that I see all the time on the Internet.

Step 1: You see a banner on the Internet that says: "Learn a Language in 10 Days."

Step 2: You click on the banner and go to a website and the first thing you read is: "Hate Learning New Languages?"

Step 3: You click to buy, and on the order page the product is called: "How to Learn Spanish in 30 Days."

OK, let's look at what happened here.

First, the main benefit I liked and why I clicked on the banner was "Learn a Language in 10 Days." This is a great headline, but when I click through, I see "Hate Learning New Languages?"

Right away, I just hit a "dry spot" on a slip and slide, because it approaches the topic in a different way. When a person clicks on a banner, the next page should always reinforce the action from the previous webpage. In this case, I should see some headline about "Learning a Language in 10 Days" so that I think I am on the right website. Why? Because I am reading about something that I just took action on.

A congruent offer would have a headline focused on the last action. When I get to step 3 to buy, again, the name of the product talks about learning Spanish in 30 days. But wait! You just told me I could learn the language in 10 days! Now, I'm off the website and you lost me as a customer forever.

Does this make sense?

Always match the action someone takes with a first view to reflect the last action. The message should stay the same. If I test an ad and find one ad with a headline that gets a 300 percent higher response rate, I should use this headline throughout the process till I am at my end goal.

Congruency is key. Your message must be the same. First, test and get the right message. Then, make sure all is congruent. Master this fundamental and you will put yourself light-years ahead of your competitors. You'll be able to look at what a competitor is making money with and take that same idea and dominate the market 100 percent.

If you aren't congruent, you lose. One day, I was checking some stats on a new campaign I launched the previous day that focused on helping people save money with coupons. I noticed an unusually high amount of traffic and no conversions—meaning tons of people were visiting the site, but no one was buying anything.

I immediately went to the advertisement we placed. I looked at our website where people came after the ad. They both looked fine. Then I looked at the keyword sending all the traffic. Ouch . . . problem found. Somehow we were bidding on the term "Facebook" and our ad headline was automatically using that keyword. So our ad actually read "Facebook."

We got tons of clicks, because the ad made us appear like we were Facebook.com. Since the title read "Facebook," that's what the searcher thought it was. By 9 a.m., I had spent about $1,200 on clicks and had $0 in return. Why? The keyword didn't match the offer of what we were selling. It was a costly mistake that anyone can make when using the "copy and paste" method of using keywords in marketing. We will discuss this more in Chapter 5.

Always check your offer from start to finish. Make sure all parts are congruent. If not, you will be dominated by better marketers.

Affiliate Marketing

Earlier, we discussed traffic and a form of traffic called affiliate marketing. I want to make sure you understand this concept.

Affiliate marketing is really simple. The beauty of it is that you do not have to own a product or offer a service just to make serious money off it. The Internet is overflowing with people and companies who already have products and services. It is only a matter of finding them and helping them grow their business by sending traffic to their websites.

Countless companies are looking for people — affiliates — who will promote their product or service online in exchange for a fee. Usually these owners of products and services go to affiliate networks, like clickbank.com, cj.com, or clickbooth.com, among many others, to help find affiliates, or they have their own affiliate program.

If you go to Walmart.com, and scan the bottom menu on the website, you will see the words "Affiliate Program." Walmart will actually pay you for sending people to their website.

Here's a little secret. If you sign up for their affiliate program, they will also pay you for buying off their website. You just become an affiliate. You don't even have to have a website. They give you a link. You click on the link and buy what you would normally buy and they'll pay you!

I do this for almost any purchase online. If you do this, you could easily pay for this book and save up to hundreds and thousands of dollars over the next one to two years. Anytime you go to buy online, look for their affiliate program. Sign up and then buy through your own link. This may not make much sense now. My advice is to just go do it once. You'll be hooked and want to save on anything you ever buy.

You have two choices when it comes to approaching affiliate marketing. The first one is what newbies do and what average Internet marketers do. The other one is what Internet millionaires do. Which one do you think you would like to learn?

All right. I was talking about a system earlier. Now let us expand on it a bit more.

Reverse Online Profits™

Reverse Online Profits™ is a system I have developed over the past five years that has generated more than $20 million in sales online. You don't need a product or a service of your own to work on this. It fits any industry and any product or service. It just works!

The simple application of this system will allow you to

- Find markets making money;

- Quickly penetrate these money-making markets and win big;

- Cut your failure rate by up to 90 percent;

- Generate leads and cash like clockwork; and

- Continue to work as the Internet keeps changing and evolving.

This strategy is centered on the old saying, "Don't try to reinvent the wheel."

I had used this strategy in my marriage. I found some people with some incredible marriages and simply did what they told me they did to have a great marriage.

I didn't grow up learning about how to have a great marriage, because my parents separated several times when I was a kid. They eventually got a divorce during my senior year of high school. So watching them was not going to give me the right formula for success in marriage.

But I knew I could have a great marriage. I just needed to figure out how to do it, to seek out successful couples, and talk to them. Now, my wife and I have an incredible marriage.

I did the same thing in raising my kids. I struggled for years with being a successful parent. Then one day, I figured out I would ask my friends how they raised their kids. Their families were amazing. These were the kinds of families where you watch the kids and think, "The parents must have just gotten lucky." But when I did some digging, I discovered it wasn't luck at all, but specific steps that worked.

Why would my success on the Internet be any different?

I spent years learning from a variety of self-described experts. However, what I found out later was that most of them were horrible at actually making money online. Failure's a bad formula to emulate.

I was sitting at my computer after months of failure, stuck and frustrated. Then, it hit me. Why not just look at what others are doing successfully online and do what they are doing?

I know this sounds simple, but it made sense. All I had learned up to that point was about massive trial and error.

And without much experience or success under my belt, it resulted in mainly massive error.

Five steps to Reverse Online Profits™

Allow me to present to you the FIVE STEPS TO REVERSE ONLINE PROFITS™:

- Find a money website or market

- Recreate the offer

- Replicate traffic

- Build a list

- Ramp and bank and go from the top again

Sounds simple enough, right?

The rest of this book will center around how to use this system to grow your business. I will walk you through each step, giving you all the secrets, tips, and strategies we use to make our computers spit out money. You will learn each step in detail in the coming chapters.

Now let me emphasize this to you again: if you want to be successful online (or offline), don't start out trying to be original. In fact, even if you run a large company, I would invest most of my time into looking into what is working and focusing my efforts there. Online success is simply a matter of taking what works and applying it effectively to your business, got that?

One final thought.

I shared the story earlier of how I was able to make close to $7,000 the first day of launching a campaign focused on weight loss. What I didn't tell you was that within 48 hours, I had five competitors. And each of these competitors squashed what I was doing. They were professionals. I was a newbie. I was still learning. I didn't know all the secrets I am sharing with you in this book.

I basically got sucker-punched by five competitors, while they ran off with thousands of dollars. I was left licking my wounds trying to figure out what happened, and who hit me.

I came up with a saying to describe the experience:

NEWBIES GET CRUSHED.

It's a harsh reality. If you do come up with a new idea and it actually does work, watch out. Your competitors will eat you alive if you are not prepared. This applies to all companies, large and small.

Take time to master the fundamentals. Learn the basics. Keep the basics in front of you at all times. Remind yourself often. Write down these principles and put them on your wall. Put them where you won't forget. Put them where you will think about them and master them.

CHAPTER 2
Find Money-Making Websites

Wouldn't you love to buy a piece of land for pennies on the dollar, then find out the day after you bought it that your land had a huge oil reserve on it? And you could start pumping thousands of gallons a day immediately?

That would be a great scenario for almost anyone. (As long as you don't mind someone giving you cash.) But it probably won't happen for you or me at any point in our lifetimes.

However, the equivalent does exist online. You can find a "piece of land" online to earn you boatloads of cash for life. You can find real estate loaded with oil, and you can own as much as you'd like.

Here's some background on how I see the Internet: I view every website as a piece of land. It literally is "real estate." In my office, this is how we refer to websites and marketing. We are 100 percent focused on finding the best real estate online and owning as much of that real estate as we can.

I see the front page of Google as real estate. I see Facebook ads as real estate. I see websites as real estate. When I find a site that has oil on it, I do all I can to own that real estate for pennies on the dollar.

This is why the first step in the Reverse Online Profits™ system is so important. It allows you to find websites, traffic, and products or services that are already making money (already pumping oil).

Target a Hungry Market

Remember one of the Millionaire Marketing eFundamentals from Chapter 1. Find a hungry market and create a product, service, or offer to sell to the ready market. It's fairly easy to do online. I've used this concept for years to draw millions and millions of valuable visitors to my websites. I've created hundreds of websites—real estate—that overflow with profits.

In 2000, I had a client who wanted me to create leads for attorney services. Let me define what a lead is before we go on. (Stick with me if you already know.) A lead is simply someone who has raised his or her hand and expressed interest in what you are offering. There are several types of leads, some are much more qualified than others, but that is a discussion for another time. The important thing is to understand that a lead is someone who has taken some action (filled out a form, called your company, etc.) and said, "Hey, I'm interested in what you have."

Back to my story: so in 2000 I had a client who wanted leads of people looking for legal help. For months, we tested everything we could to create leads and just couldn't get the leads the client needed. It was very frustrating. I was already doing all I knew how to do.

One day, I decided to look at a website focused on aiding people who need legal help. I filled out a form on its page so I could get a call from its operator. When the person called me, I first asked, "How did you get my information?" The sales representative told me how: they had bought this lead (me) from a lead-generation marketing company.

Then, I went to a company to buy leads of people looking for legal services. They delivered leads to me. As soon as I got a lead, I called the person and asked how he or she found me. To my surprise, the leads told me the exact websites. Some of the people even told me if they found me on a search engine, like Google, they told me which keyword they typed in Google to find me. In other words, they told me what they were searching for on Google so I knew the keywords which were driving results. So I got a ton of information about which websites the leads were coming from and the keywords they may have typed in (if they used a search engine).

I then turned around and created a website like the one the leads had visited to find "me." (It wasn't actually "me" they were finding; it was the lead-generation company's website, but the leads don't understand this, so it was easier to ask how they found me.) This way, the website was based on the one that was already working.

Long story short. Within the next few months, I went from frustrated, not being able to create any leads, and not able to get any good traffic, to creating up to 20,000 to 30,000 leads a month. It worked so well that I started a business of not only selling these leads, but also found out how I could get leads for my own company to sell legal services.

We put close to 30,000 people onto these legal services within the next twelve to twenty-four months and generated millions and millions of dollars in revenue.

That's the power of the first step of the Reverse Online Profits™ system. Find a money website. Do the research. Make money. It can be this simple. It will set you up for success in anything you do online.

If you have an existing business, this concept works just as well, and in many cases, is even more powerful. You will use this first step to dissect exactly what is bringing revenue to your competitors so you can focus on this and blow them out of the water. You will get so good at this that you will know more about the sources of competitors' revenue than they do. Once you know this, they will waste money buying advertising that doesn't work, while you succeed with the advertising that does work.

This is where you start to "own the block," as I call it. When you get this chapter down, you will not only find money websites, you will start to own the block. You can take over!

Now, my team and I are able to find keywords that work so well for different products and services we work with that we actually go into a search engine and own most of the first page.

We don't just have a goal to get a great position on the front page of Google or on a page on Facebook. We own as much of that page as we can get, often running our competitors out of the market.

That's total domination of the market!

I love to look at money sites we create and then look at the market and see our numbers skyrocket, while the other websites' traffic plummets. You will learn how to totally dominate any market, any product, or any service as you continue through this book.

This first step is a critical one. This is where I spend most of my time. I focus on finding winning markets, winning products, and winning services, and then crank out new strategies to dominate these markets and websites.

Let's take a look at where we are in the process of going through the Reverse Online Profits™ system.

Are you ready to learn more about step 1?
Let's get into it.

Find the Money Websites

I like the color green. Do you like the color green? I like it, because it means go and cash. Does that make sense to you? Go & Cash. It's pretty exciting actually. But before you can find the cash, you need to do market research to find out where the money is going. Then you can tap that gold vein to get your money.

To find the money websites, you have to consider what I call the Green Light System, which represents Go & Cash. I will talk about this system in depth in the next chapter, but I want you to keep it in mind when researching websites to find the money-makers.

The system begins with finding the money websites, because, as I have mentioned, finding a website or offer that is already successfully doing what you want is the place to start. You just have to find these money-makers. So if your goal is to make a million dollars, naturally the first step is to find the websites that are already making a million dollars! Easy! If you want to sell dog food, find a site already successful in selling dog food. If you sell a widget, find a website already successfully selling widgets.

I want to define what a "keyword" is, if you don't already know. A keyword is simply a phrase or word that you or anyone else types into Google or any search engine to find something. For example, if I am looking for a karate school for my kids, I might type "karate school" on the Google website.

There are two main types of keywords: short tail and long tail keywords.

Short tail keywords are basically keyword searches of one to two words in a phrase. This is like the example above of "karate school." An example of a long tail keyword would be "karate school in south Austin." This search phrase has five words in it.

It's important to know all this terminology when starting to learn about how to use search engines to make money.

Let's go through a brief overview of some strategies to find money websites, and then we'll dive deeper into each method.

Tools to Find Money Websites

- Use search engines, like Google, Yahoo, and Bing, to search for keywords.

- Use the Google Keyword tool to see how many times the keyword is typed in. (To find this, simply go to Google.com and search for "Google keyword tool." It will be the top listing on Google.com.)

1. Log in to Facebook (now this is a great way to use Facebook) and add to your "likes" the competitor or comparable market.

2. Here's how this works. Log in to your Facebook account and then do a search for any type of group or person. For example, let's say I wanted to find out who was advertising to real estate people in my area. I might do a search to find a local Facebook group. Or maybe there is a Realtor's association in my city or even in my state.

3. Once I find the group, I simply click the icon "like" on their page. Then I will start to see ads of people targeting real estate agents. Make sense? Find a fan page or group in Facebook and "like" them. Next, keep your eyes on your ads and see how they change. You will quickly see ads targeted at this new "like."

-   Talk to your affiliate manager (if you are in affiliate marketing) and ask for information.

    1. If you are working as an affiliate for any company, product, or service, or an affiliate network — like CJ.com, Clickbooth.com, or others listed at JeffUsner.com™ — you can ask the affiliate manager what is working best. You can also ask what is working best on search engines, Facebook, etc.

-   Research blogs and forums.

-   Take a competitor website and use compete.com or keywordspy.com.

Now, let's go into more detail about how to do each of these steps.

Look up Keywords

One of the most important things that you have to do first, before you launch any project or product, is doing a keyword search in search engines. But what everyone does not know is how to do it in a way that you can make money and dominate the market in the best and most effective way possible.

Keywords are powerful. Keywords are what drive the largest revenues in online spending.

When I first started promoting a weight-loss product, I discovered one keyword that generated over $20,000 in commissions in the first week! From one keyword.

Keywords are like gold. Once you find keywords that work, keywords that convert visitors to paid clients on your product, service, or company, you literally can guarantee ongoing high-quality people coming to your business. So keywords are critical when looking for money websites.

When you want to know which sites are making money, you can use Google, Yahoo, Bing or any other search engine. The task is to:

- Do a keyword search on a topic or market;

- Look at websites/competitors in your market;

- Search a competitor's domain by typing in "the domain you want to look at";

- Look at long tail keywords;

- Look up keywords and see who is advertising on the keyword;

- Look at ads appearing on each keyword search.

Let's walk through an example of this.

Step 1: Go to Google.com.

Step 2: Let's begin to type a word in the search box for a market we are interested in.

Let's say we are in the weight-loss business and we want to work with people looking to lose weight. Ask yourself: What words would these people type into Google? If they are looking to lose weight, they may type in "lose weight" (short tail keyword) or "lose weight fast within the next 10 days" (this is a long tail keyword, because it's got many more words).

For this example, I want you to start typing in "lose weight fast," but just type in the word "lose" to start. Then look at what shows up in the drop-down menu.

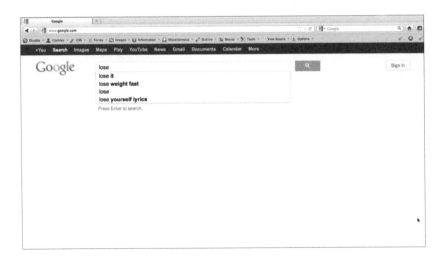

As you can see, Google "pre-populates" terms that we searched for, based on searches done by other people who type the same word while doing a search.

So when we research, Google helps us think of other key-words or phrases that people use during similar searches.

Let's continue and type "lose weight fast" and see what Google does.

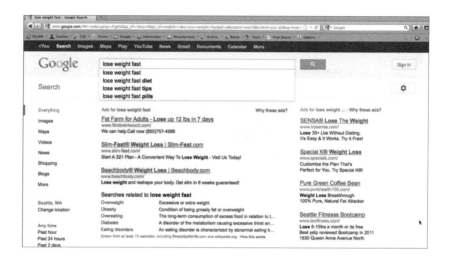

As you can see, Google is still trying to help with our search by showing the terms:

"Lose weight fast"
"Lose weight fast diet"
"Lose weight fast tips"
"Lose weight fast pills"

This is market research. This is valuable information we are starting to gather from Google. This is telling us other words/phrases that people looking to lose weight are typing. Many times, I will write these words down to reference later in our research. I discover some amazing secrets about my marketplace from just Google pre-populating terms like above. You will too!

Look at the previous screen shot again. I want to point out a few other pieces of valuable information you now have.

- Look at the ads that show up in the little tan-colored box at top of the search results, just under the search box. Everything listed in this tan box and on the far right are people/businesses that are paying Google to show up there prominently. They got there, because they paid for the space and position.

- Below the tan box are other words used for searches similar to "lose weight fast." Again, Google is giving us some valuable information on other words our target market is typing in and other words they are concerned with and looking for help with. This is great for helping us to find a hungry market and what they want to buy.

- You also are getting some valuable information by looking more closely at the ads showing up for your keywords. Make a note of the domains that are paying Google to show up in this keyword search.

The good news with this search is we see people are spending money to advertise to our potential market or the market we are already advertising to. You will do some searches and not find any advertisers, and many times this is not necessarily a good thing, because it likely means that keyword is not making anyone any money. It can also start to show you that the market you are considering going into doesn't have much of a demand.

Remember, let the market tell you what it wants to buy, not what you think it wants to or should buy. You will make a lot more money focused on your market and what it does, instead of trying to figure it out with your own ideas.

From the previous search, we have learned there is a lot of competition for the words "lose weight fast." What websites do we see advertising?

Here are a few:

www.fixrxbrentwood.com
www.slim-fast.com
www.beachbody.com
www.trysensa.com
www.specialk.com

These are the top listings that get most of the traffic, because they fall in the top five. The top five listings usually get over 85 percent of the clicks. So for this research, let's focus on them.

Step 3: Do a Google Search for the domain of someone advertising on your keyword phrase.

Let's search for the domain www.slim-fast.com and see what we find out:

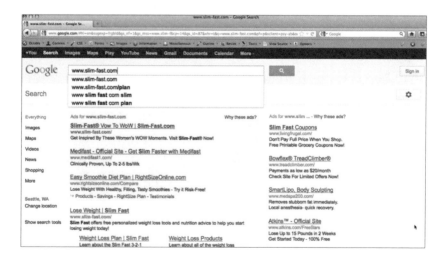

When we search for a term from one of the advertisers, we will often learn some more information. In this case, we see there are many advertisers paying Google to show up for a search on www.slim-fast.com.

We also see from the pre-populated drop-down search results that many people who type in www.slim-fast.com also type in www.slim-fast.com/plan. This is interesting and means we could also bid in Google's system on the keyword www.slim-fast.com/plan and get highly targeted traffic to our website.

When we see people bidding on someone else's domain name (their website address), this means this site (in this case www.slim-fast.com) is a proven player in the market. Again, you may not be in the weight-loss business, but understand this applies in any market. Remember, we are looking for websites that are already successfully doing what we want to do. This will cut out a ton of trial-and-error attempts and help us to succeed wildly with our business.

Step 4: Let's get more information on how big our market could be. Let's go to Google.com and type "Google keyword tool." The top listing should be Google.com/(something about keyword tool). Let's click on it. The result should look something like this:

In the box that says "Word or phrase," let's type "lose weight fast."

Google will reveal how many times this term has been used in searches, as well as other terms people type when searching in this market. In this case, we see that "lose weight fast" (on a broad search — I'll explain this more later) shows up in 1,220,000 searches a month. That's a lot of searches.

It means there is a huge market looking for what we are thinking of offering.

For this example, we are using a rather large market in weight loss. In your market, the search volume could be much less. We are looking for words with more than 5,000 to 10,000 monthly searches to show us there is a real market to go after.

With our first four steps of research in Google, we've discovered there is a lot of competition in our market and there are a lot of people looking for our market. These are two big bonuses for us! (I'll cover this in depth in the next chapter.)

Another method to research a market is to simply Google the phrase of the market you are in and add the word "forum" or "blog" at the end of it. For example, let's stay in weight loss and Google "weight loss blog."

We find many blogs talking about weight loss. We can go to these websites to see what our market is talking about and find out what it wants and what it's looking for. Let's visit one of these sites.

The top listing appearing in our search is MyAllNatural-WeightLoss.com. Go to this website now.

The first thing I see on this website is ads on the right side of the page. When I look around on the site, I discover that below the ads is a link that says "advertise here." So I have found a site I could buy advertising on (we'll discuss this later). I also can now click on the ads from the people already paying money to be on this website to see what they are selling to this market.

Does this make sense?

We are finding people who are already marketing to our market or our potential market. We are finding some good signs of competition and see others succeeding in their marketing.

We could read through this blog and find out other possible keywords people are talking about and what problems they have that we could help solve. (Remember, your goal is to find the hungry market and solve its problems.)

Again, this works for any market, so let's take a quick look at another market. Say, for example, you are a dog trainer. The target market is on "dog training." Let's say you love dogs and want to create a product focused on training dogs.

You could create a product or a service to help people train their dog. If you research further, you would see there is a large market for people looking to house-break their dogs. You could cater to any of these markets by creating a product to help solve this problem.

Actually, you don't have to create the product, such as an e-book, yourself. You can pay someone to write a book about it or maybe do a video series on dog training, and that is it. You don't even have to know how to train a dog.

Maybe you just like dogs and that is enough really. You can hire someone from the Philippines (I will tell you how to do this later) and pay a couple hundred bucks and in a few weeks, you will have your dog training material that can be better or is comparable to what is already out there in the market.

Long Tail Keywords

I want to emphasize that long tail keywords are money. When you type in Google and look for ideas, make sure you shoot for the long tail keywords, because you can make some serious money with them. It is what all the pros do. It is what all the Internet Millionaires do.

Remember that long tail keywords are gold (for example, "weight loss" is a short tail keyword; "how to lose 15 lbs in 20 days" is a long tail keyword.)

Facebook

The best way to use Facebook for market research and to find money websites, offers, services, and products is to simply monitor the ads you see in Facebook. Once you are logged into your account, you can go to facebook.com/ads/adboard to look for ads targeted at you. They are targeted at your interests, your age, your gender, your relationship status, and much more. (You'll learn how to use this later in this book.)

Once you have seen what people are advertising to you, you can set up other Facebook accounts with varying demographics just to get to know what other marketers are serving these people. They can include the following characteristics:

- Male/female
- Age group: 18-25, 26-35, 35-50, 50+
- Single, married, kids
- Likes, interests, schools attended

Then you can do the following:

- Monitor what ads show up
- Look at the "likes" of leaders/gurus/celebs

You can even tailor your Facebook accounts to suit the market that you are trying to target. For example, if you are looking at the dog-training market, you could add different types of dogs to your "likes" in your interests on Facebook. Then, you could see what ads are displayed on the right side of your Facebook account, or you can go directly to Facebook ad boards (facebook.com/ads/adboard) and see what Internet marketers are showing people who like dogs. I added a dog to one of my "likes" and the first ad I saw was for a doggie diaper!

Become a student of marketing. Learn to watch ads displayed to you and try to figure out why they were displayed to you. When you see ads, click on them and see what other people are doing. Ask yourself how you can do it or how you can do it better. What are the needs that are not being fulfilled?

All of these are crucial questions when it comes to market research, and once you have gotten it all down, it is all about entering the market and dominating it!

Think Laterally

Remember Millionaire Business Concept No. 1: always think laterally. You can do this for any market, any product, or any service. For example, if you search for dog clothing, you will see sites for dog clothes for July 4th. What if you come up with dog wear for Christmas, Valentine's Day, or Thanksgiving? Or, think about what else you could market to people targeted around the July 4th holiday.

Before you know it, you will have a good money-making business that is raking in money for you every month of every year. Every year when a holiday comes around, you have all these people looking for your website, willing and wishing and able to give you money every time. How simple is that?

Find Your Niche

You can even go into specific niches and offer the same thing but target more customers by being specific. For instance, you could market dog clothing specifically for large dogs, toy dogs, dogs of sports fans, dogs of Nascar fans, dogs of fraternity people, or whatever. With this simple technique alone, you can make lots of money. It is all about applying the concept to your business, generating tons of ideas, picking one that works, and putting it into action.

Tap the Goldmine of Ideas

So now you have a goldmine of ideas in front of you. Go to these websites and have a good look at what the other marketers are doing. What is their headline? What does their landing page look like? Opt in to their forms, buy their stuff, and subscribe to their offers/emails. If you really want to get into a niche, you have to get in there and learn what other people are doing, duplicate that, improve on it, and do it. It is really that simple.

Tips on subscriptions: If you are going to subscribe (opt in) to someone else's newsletters or information forms, make sure you use a separate email account, because you don't want your personal account to be cluttered with all these incoming emails, which can be a huge distraction.

You need to stay focused.

Find the Money Market

With the entire five-step system of Reverse Online Profits™, the most important concept is naturally the first one: find the money website, find the money market. Basically, you want to find something that makes money that is similar to what you want to do, similar to what you are trying to accomplish, or trying to get into.

Getting ideas is simple and easy. There is no excuse not to come up with a clever idea for your business, because simply following this process will yield tons of ideas. You do not even have to do it yourself; you can hire someone else to do it for you. You can just say that you are looking for some ideas, give instructions, and tell the person to follow the steps in this chapter. Then see what he or she finds, and take action. Making money is really this simple.

For example, if you are into widgets, you can find a successful widget-selling company and run their website through this system and, if they are making money, simply duplicate or replicate what they are trying to do and go make money. Literally, this system can be applied to anything out there. Online, offline, ANYTHING!

Next up, in Chapter 3, we will take an in-depth look at the Green Light System to see how to apply it to prospective money-making websites that you have found using the tools and tips in this chapter.

Here are some bonus research tools you can use to find and come up with new ideas:

- Alexa.com

- Trendwatching.com/trends

- Squidoo.com/browse/top_lenses

- Quantcast.com

- Google.com/trends

- Buzz.yahoo.com (great for pay-per-view (ppv), Facebook ads)

- KeywordSpy.com

CHAPTER 3
Green Light System

In the last 20 years of my business and personal life, I can't even begin to count the number of ideas I've acted on that have failed miserably. It didn't matter whether it was a way to create a website, an advertisement in a major U.S. publication, radio commercials, products, software, e-books, sales strategies, deciding on an employee, deciding on a business relationship, deciding on what to do with my kids, making a mistake while driving, making a mistake while talking (foot in mouth), or in any aspect of my life. Mistakes followed more mistakes. Failure after failure.

I still make tons of mistakes. I say "sorry" more than I'd like to. This is because I am an action taker. I get an idea and just go. This happens a lot in every area of life.

Have you ever made a mistake in your life? How about this year? Today maybe? We all make mistakes, but what if before you ever acted on an idea, you had a system that would show you green lights to indicate when to go and red lights to tell you when to stop?

Would this help you avoid some mistakes? Some collisions?

Of course it would.

This is exactly why I developed the Green Light System. It is an almost foolproof way to practically guarantee, or at least increase, your chances of succeeding by up to 500 percent or more.

Would you be interested in a system like this?

I know I would.

I would go back to some of the business decisions I made and put them through a system where I'd know if it was a "red light" to start. I would never have put my foot on the gas to go down the road to the eventual disasters I've had online.

The first month I put the Green Light System into action in my business, I made almost $36,000. Since then, I've used this system to launch hundreds of websites and ideas in multiple businesses to create millions of dollars with hardly any failure. This method ensured that up to 90 percent or more of the websites or ideas we have acted on are profitable.

Imagine being in Las Vegas with 90 percent odds in your favor? You might gamble a little more aggressively. You might do some things you might not normally do. You would be setting yourself up for a big win.

That's what this system does. And it works in any economy, in any market, and in any circumstance, even as the Internet continues to change.

Understand the Green Light System you are about to learn is a key component of step 1 of the Reverse Online Profits™ five-step system. This is where you can make and save a lot of money and time. It's one of the most valuable systems you will ever use online.

Let's review where you are in the Reverse Online Profits™ system. The Green Light System is a critical part of step 1.

Green Light Means Go & Go Means Cash!

The idea is to apply the following four Green Lights to the possible money-making websites or ideas that have grabbed your attention.

- High traffic

- Consistent traffic

- Multiple search engines or media sources

- Replication ready or easy to duplicate

Let's walk through each one of these Green Lights so you can understand how to use them in your business to drive more traffic, make more money, and get more buyers.

Green Light # 1: High Traffic

After going through the last chapter, you should now have a few ideas of websites about a business you like. Or maybe you just found a website implementing one new business idea you'd like to use to grow your business. Either way, let's take that website and start to put it through the Green Light System.

The first Green Light indicator is to check the website and see if it is getting traffic. If there are no visitors to the website, that would be a huge red light to heed.

There are many ways that you can check to see if other websites have high traffic or not. One way that I highly recommend is using Compete.com. I will explain in a moment how to do this. If you find that a website is getting a lot of traffic, and the website owners are paying for this traffic, this usually means they are making money. Make sense? You don't normally spend money on advertising unless you are getting a good return on your investment.

You can find out if website owners are paying for the traffic that Compete.com shows you by simply visiting those websites and seeing if the ads are paid for: Are they banners? Are they in the paid search listings on Google.com? Those are some indicators.

The No. 1 tool/website I use every day is <u>Compete.com</u>. I believe it's the best resource to get competitive information on any website. The free version of Compete.com will give you enough information to determine the Green Lights and when to go on. If you want to invest in the paid versions of Compete, I'll share with you a way I discovered to get access at a great price.

How to Use Compete.com

Go to compete.com and type in the domain/website you found in your market research in the last chapter.

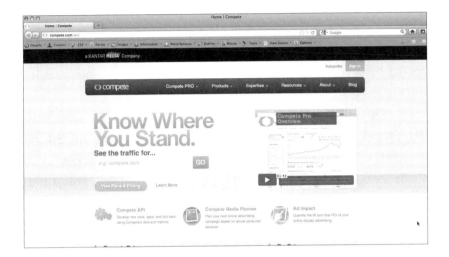

For example, let's use the website I found on Google when researching "dog training." It is www.thedogtrainingsecret.com. Let's look at what Compete.com has to say about this site.

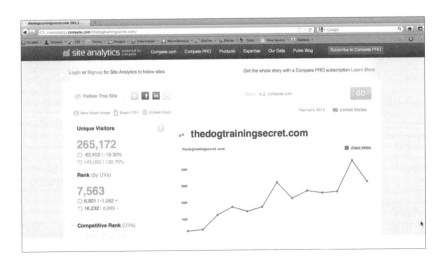

The first Green Light in the Green Light System is "high traffic." I see the traffic the site got last month was 265,172 unique visitors. The question then is: Is that high traffic? The answer will depend on your market.

If you have a business where you are already getting 2 million unique visitors to your website each month, then 265,172 visitors may not be a lot of people. However, it still could be a lot of people if this were a potential new niche you were going to go after in your market.

Let's say you have a huge list of dog owners who buy dog food from you. Then the 265,172 visitors might be enough traffic for you to consider entering the market.

If you have a business where you have less than 1,000 visitors a month to your website, then 265,172 unique visitors in a month is a lot! If you can just capture a tenth of the traffic of this site, you could have a good profitable business on your hand.

Whether you consider a site is a high-traffic one depends on you and your business. For me, if a website is getting more than 5,000 to 10,000 visitors a month in an average-sized market, it means we could probably develop an income of $3,000 to $8,000 a month. Again, this depends on the vertical or market your are entering. If I have a luxury yacht business and I get 10,000 visitors a month, that traffic might be very high and could be worth $1 million a month.

Everything is relative to the market you are in. However, as a general rule, if a site is getting 5,000 to 10,000 visitors a month, it could be a good market if your income goal was $3,000 to $8,000 a month. If you are just starting a new business, 5,000 to 10,000 visitors a month can be a good business.

High traffic is dependent on your market and your goals. The key is to figure out if the traffic is enough for you to invest time into going after this market and/or if this website you found is a good competitor or player in your desired market.

Let's say in this example, the traffic (265,172 unique visitors) is high traffic. This website would pass the test of Green Light No. 1.

Let's move on to see if it is a go on Green Light No. 2.

Green Light #2: Consistent Traffic

Let's look at the <u>www.thedogtrainingsecret.com</u> site again on Compete.com.

You can see there is steady traffic flowing to this site. In fact, it's mostly an upward trend. Finding a site with an upward trend is an added green light and go signal, but is not necessary for the primary Green Light System.

However, I'd rather enter markets that are in an upward swing. The key is to have consistent traffic. You might find a site that passes Green Light No. 1 (high traffic), but if it is not consistent or if it's brand new, then you will want to approach it with caution.

It's best to find a site that is green on the first four Green Lights before we proceed. Consistent web traffic is key to any business. Look at how many months the traffic has been consistent. As a rule, always look for at least four to six months of consistent traffic to know if the website passes this Green Light.

I like to enter markets where once I set up the website, products, and systems (all that goes into whatever market we are entering) the company/site can make money consistently without having to keep going back and coming up with new ideas to promote it.

I like businesses that grow and grow after I do the initial work. So high traffic and consistent traffic are the first two Green Lights to look for.

Let's move on to Green Light No. 3.

Green Light #3: Multiple Search Engines or Media Sources

When you find a website with high traffic and consistent traffic, it's time to see if this website or business has been growing in other media. The key here is if we find a website spending money to advertise on Google, Yahoo, Facebook, and other websites, we know this website is making money if Green Lights No. 1 and No. 2 are also a go.

Why? Because if someone is spending money across many verticals, it means their offer or website is very well crafted and making money. Green Light No. 3 is a biggie. When we get the Green Light on this one, it's go time!

Let's look at the example of TheDogTrainingSecret.com. First let's go to Google.com.

Sure enough, if we look at the top ad on the right side of the screen, we see TheDogTrainingSecret.com advertising on Google.

Ok, let's check out Yahoo.com.

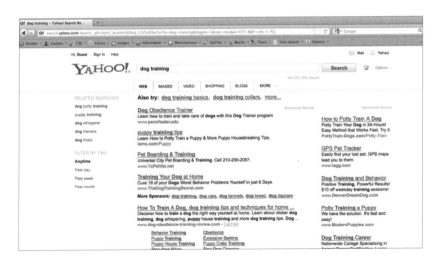

The fourth listing on Yahoo is the site, with the headline "Training Your Dog at Home," from TheDogTrainingSecret. com.

We've confirmed that this website is paying for traffic from Google and Yahoo. That's two media sources, and it passes the test of Green Light No. 3.

We could also go to our Facebook.com page and under the "Add Interests" section, we could add different breeds of dogs. We could then go to Facebook.com/ads/adboard or just look on our screen to see which ads will appear.

This strategy with Facebook works best if you haven't listed a lot of interests in your account. If you have a lot of interests, there will be more advertisers competing to have their ad in front of you. So if you get a Facebook account for checking ads, fewer interests is the best approach.

For this example on TheDogTrainingSecret.com, I have seen enough. This website is paying for traffic from Google and Yahoo. Green Light No. 3 is a go!

We now have a go on Green Light No. 1 (high traffic), on No. 2 (consistent traffic), and now on No. 3 (advertising on multiple locations). This is definitely a market that is making money. We could start to build a similar product and marketing funnel, and have a great opportunity for a highly profitable business.

Important note: If a website doesn't pass the test on Green Light No. 3, it does not necessarily mean that we don't go into the market. On the contrary, it can mean more opportunity.

Frankly, most Internet marketers do not make sure that they are represented on multiple search engines, because they do not know about the importance of Green Light No. 3. So what can you do with this information?

Say for example, you find a website in Google or a niche that you want to get into, and it is not on other search engines like Yahoo or Bing or 7search or whatever. Guess what that means? INSTANT CASH! You can just run the Green Light

System and do what that person is doing and make money.

If, for example, we see someone is getting a lot of traffic from Google, but not from Yahoo or Bing, this means we could possibly just become an affiliate for this person and drive traffic from Yahoo and Bing and make money.

When you find a competitor, keep in mind the following websites, which will help you decide if the competing website has the Green Lights or not:

- Keywordspy.com (Green Lights 1 and 2)

- Quantcast.com (Green Lights 1 and 2)

- Alexa.com (Green Lights 1 and 2)

- Compete.com (Green Lights 1, 2, and 3)

So if you see a website that has high traffic and consistent traffic, it is all a matter of duplicating that traffic. We'll talk about that in an upcoming chapter.

Let's move on to Green Light No. 4.

Green Light #4: Replication Ready or Easy to Duplicate

Once you find a website that is green on at least the first two Green Lights, it's time to see if it will be green on the last one.

Here's how you check. Once you have identified a potential winner, I want you to spend some time on its website. Is this a website you could create? Is this a product or service you could offer? (The answer to these questions may change once you learn in later chapters how to have all of this done without you having to do any writing, creating a product or website!)

Click on one of the ads of the websites you are considering. We want to see the website and see if it is easy to duplicate. With our example for the dog training, it is quite simple. If you look at it, you can tell that the person who owns this website knows what he or she is doing. (You will learn more about what makes a winning offer or website in the next chapter.)

If you look at the dog-training website (please don't click on their ad so they don't get charged; go to http://www.thedogtrainingsecret.com/tips to see the page they are advertising), this website has good marketing elements. We'll discuss this in depth in the next chapter. For now, just notice there is a good video, a place to get more information and give your email address, and much more. It's a good site. And it would be easy to create a site similar to it.

So let's run the four Green Lights on this website:

- It has high traffic

- It has consistent traffic

- It is on multiple mediums (It's on Google and Yahoo)

- It is pretty simple to replicate

BOOM!

That's it. Four Green Lights. This site is a winner! Get out there and make money. How simple can simple be, right? The Green Lights can be used in any type of product or service on the Internet. This system can be used on new businesses or existing businesses.

I'd like to make a quick point about Green Light No. 4. Do not think when you find a winning combination that you need to create the product every time to make money.

Money-Making Ideas

Here are some other ideas on how to make money from this market research and money website we found.

First, if we found out that an advertiser was not on other advertising mediums — such as other search engines, media buys, Facebook, or other websites — we could simply become an affiliate and go send traffic to this site and see if we can make money. This website may not be buying all the media they could to make money. So if we just did this, we could cash in.

Second, we could make money without having to create any product. We just set up the ads, choose the keywords (by doing what I'll teach you later), and send the same traffic to a competitor of this website. If the competitor has an affiliate program and will send us traffic, then maybe that's all we do.

We don't even have to build a website; we could just send the competitor traffic and make money from the affiliate link.

Third, we could create a free report or pay someone to do this (as I'll show you later), which we give for free to the people looking for dog training. Then, we could simply advise them to go to this exact person's website and buy the product. Now, we would want to be an affiliate of the product so that we would get paid for each sale and we would be building our list. (I'll discuss this more later, as well.) Bottom line, this is big . . . we could get paid to build a list of people who might want to buy something else we recommend in the future. There are countless ways to do this online in any market or niche.

Four, we could go find someone who has a great product but has no traffic, because they don't know how to market online. Maybe they spent a ton writing their book or creating a course on how to train a dog, but then they realized the saying "If you build it, they will come" from the movie Field of Dreams only works in the movies.

In other words, they have a great product, but they don't know how to market it. Maybe we just buy the rights to their product and sell it. Or we could say, I'll sell your book/course, and I'll pay you $10 for each sale.

Then we control the product and the back end (I'll discuss later), where all the money is really made. Give them a little piece of the front end so they make some money and we make some money, but we also have margin left over to buy advertising. Everybody wins—and we can win big time on the back end in the long term, selling web visitors other products they might be interested in.

Imagine if you could add 100 people daily to your email list and these 100 people have spent money online to buy something to train their dog. After a month, you might have about 3,000 people to talk to about other dog products/services. After a year, you might have close to 40,000 or more people, and within a few years you may have over 100,000 dog owners who have bought something on the Internet. This is a major asset that could be sold or marketed to, earning tens of thousands of dollars. And all you did was drive some traffic on the front end based on a competitor's successful traffic buys.

When you learn this Green Light System, you will have many opportunities open in front of you, because you will know how to bring any business more qualified buyers.

This is where you can have a lot of freedom in your life.

And when you do this on a search engine or Facebook or some other website, you can set it up and forget about it. I have websites that take maybe 10 hours of work a year and make us money almost three years straight. I said 10 hours a year or less. I have one website that made our company close to $50,000 a month for a long time from one-time efforts.

You can do this.

When you learn and master the Green Light System, you will set yourself up for success in any business, industry, product, or service online. You can become the person who controls the money-making traffic on the Internet.

You don't have to own your own product or service. You can use the strategies we just discussed to make a lot of money and build a big business.

(Hint: This book and new training we've developed is my first product I've actually sold online in years. This means I've made millions using the strategies I laid out for you without having to create my own product.)

I like this model because I don't have:

- Customers
- Customer support
- Billing
- Large staff
- Product creation
- Product fulfillment
- Merchant processing

- An office

- Office hours

- And much more...

You can simply build a large company focusing on web traffic. But if you want to create an offer, let's talk about how to do it in the next chapter.

Whether you have your own product or services or not, creating your own winning offer is one of the most valuable skills you can learn. It will help you convert all the traffic you'll be getting into money for life in any area of your existing business or in any new business.

Next, let's learn to create a blueprint for creating winning offers!

CHAPTER 4
Create Your Money-Making Offer

Here's how my sons, ages 6 and 7, made $25 an hour on their first day of business. Their story gives us a great example of how easy it can be to do step 2 of the Reverse Online Profits™ system to create a winning offer.

My sons love to ask questions about business. In fact, last year, they wanted to start their first business. It was a great way for them to start learning people skills, leadership skills, and business and marketing skills.

Their success gave me a great example to share with you about how step 2 of the Reverse Online Profits™ system works. It's so easy that a 6-year-old can do it.

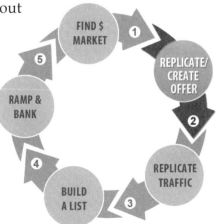

Let's recap where you are in the process and get into the story. You are in step 2. We are focused on creating your winning offer.

Back to my sons. I consulted with my sons on the best way to start a business and be successful. I took them through a few simple steps to discover what business they could succeed in and what would work best for them.

It was pretty simple. It was just five steps. As we went through the five steps, they followed to create a winning offer. Let's walk through the exact steps we took to discover what market they could sell to, what product/service they could sell to that market, and how to create an irresistible offer. (Your goal is an irresistible offer to a hungry market.)

1. Discover What People Want to Buy

The first place we started was to find a market my sons could sell to that was hungry and ready to buy something. What market did two kids have access to? This is a great question for anyone looking to enter a market. Look at what current assets you have in your life and what markets there are as you go through these steps. A 6-year-old and a 7-year-old have some limitations, but not many.

After I asked them who could they market to and what the market would be hungry to buy, my sons sat there for a while thinking about what they could do. What was in front of them? What market could they sell to? What would that market want to buy? We spent some time brainstorming ideas.

Eventually, one of them looked outside and saw the golf course. (We live on a golf course, in case you haven't figured it out.) We threw around several ideas about what they could do.

We figured out we could sell something to the golfers passing by. After all, most golfers have some expendable cash to spend. They are a buying market.

They just spent about $100 on each round of golf. What would they buy?

What would golfers (our hungry market) want to buy?

We shared some ideas, but nothing stuck. Then one of the boys said we get golf balls in our yard sometimes. And we already were going out on the course to find balls—it is one of our favorite activities to do together. Late in the evening, we will often walk down several holes and recover up to forty balls in a night. The kids love it, because it's like an Easter egg hunt! (In Texas, it's an Easter egg hunt with rattlesnakes, so we are very careful.)

So we looked at what we had in front of us to work with and found a hungry market we could sell to. We also figured out what to sell to them. Here's what we discovered.

Golfers always lose golf balls (some, including myself, more than others). So why not sell the golf balls we find on our nightly hunts? After all, we already had hundreds of balls sitting in a bucket in the garage that I would never get through.

I asked my sons, "Would people buy golf balls? Do they need golf balls?"

A huge smile lit their faces as they answered together, "Yes!" So we found the need. What's next?

2. Find a Solution

The solution to the people's need was to give them golf balls. We were also positioned where the golfers would have already played some holes and were sure to have lost a few golf balls. The need would be more apparent to them. We had this step covered. We already had hundreds of golf balls, and we could easily find a ton of golf balls walking around the course. The best part was that our cost to get the product was free. Our only investment was the time to find them. So my sons said, "Why don't we sell golf balls?"

3. Create an Irresistible Offer

The boys headed out to the garage to find the bucket of balls we already had corralled. We brought the bucket outside and began to go through the balls. We discovered we had a challenge to overcome. Most of the balls were very dirty. I asked them, "Do you think people will pay more and buy more if the balls are dirty or clean?"

"Clean," they answered.

"OK, great, let's get some rags and start cleaning!"

"But, Daddy, there's a ball cleaner right there on the tee box."

So we headed with our bucket of balls and some rags to a ball cleaner. After we had the balls shined up and looking brand new, we had to decide how to get in front of the market. How would we present our product?

Joel found an Igloo cooler to pour all the balls into. Joshua grabbed the red wagon to put the cooler on. Now, we had a good setup. We could wheel out to the golf cart path fairly easily and clean up just as easily. I liked that part! Our golf balls were shining and we had them where golfers could see them.

Part of creating an irresistible offer is to create enough value so your price point seems like a great deal. At first, we just asked for $1 each, but later we got on the Internet to investigate what golf balls sell for. We found some brands sell for a lot more than others. So we could put the nicer brands on top of the other balls. And we buried some nice balls for later. That way, people would see the nice ones (more expensive brands), which would get more of their attention. And, if they bought a bunch, we could sell the lower-perceived-value balls for more money as a package deal. The boys found all types of balls. The best and the lowest-priced. We set our price point at $1 a ball to start.

Side note: Here are three ways to increase the value of any new or existing client. We will explore these strategies in this story.

- Increase the number of customers

- Increase the initial transaction

- Increase the frequency of their purchases

To create an irresistible offer and focus on the three strategies above, we decided to initially home in on strategy No. 2 and give the golfers a discount if they bought more balls. We offered a discounted price of $5 for six balls. This increased our average sale from $1 to $5 immediately. The boys were limited to the number of customers on the golf course outside our home, so focusing on strategy No. 1 (increase the number of customers) was not as easy. We started looking at an online store to take care of this and increase our customers. And we focused on strategy #2 (increase the initial transaction). We'll discuss later how the boys also focused on strategy #3 (increase the frequency of purchase).

The boys took a piece of cardboard and wrote, "Golf balls for sale: $1 each or six balls for $5" to make a sign.

To help make our offer irresistible, we began to position their golf-ball stand as the place to go for golf balls. One of the strategies we followed was to tape some new golf ball boxes to their cardboard sign in case people had a hard time reading from afar a sign written by two young elementary school students. The message was a lot clearer then. Golfers could see the balls, the sign, and the golf ball boxes. Plus, we used higher-brand golf ball boxes on the sign, associating all our products as good-quality golf balls. The message was starting to get clear. But would it work? Would our offer be irresistible?

The boys wheeled the Igloo cooler out to the golf cart path and attached the sign. Because the balls were on a wagon (and at times on a small table), there were a few benefits:

1. The sign was higher, which made it easier to read. Our market could see our message.

2. It was more presentable and professional.

3. Our pricing was clear.

4. Our offer was clear.

The boys were all ready to make some money in their business.

"Secret Sauce" Elements

This year, we will work into my sons' offer two more elements: scarcity and urgency. These are two of the most powerful marketing elements to motivate people to take action. In any offer you create, you want to involve scarcity and urgency so people don't think the product or service is going to be around forever.

In marketing, here are a few classic scarcity tactics you have probably seen:

- "While supplies last"

- "First 50 shoppers"

- "Available till 8 p.m. tonight"

When you use scarcity and urgency in your marketing, you force people to make a decision. The fear of loss is a powerful motivator to include in any message.

4. Take Action, Adjust, Adapt

The boys took action and started out with the offer described above. Their first few customers drove right by them. They had a problem.

Most of the people would smile, wave, and drive by.

Joshua asked, "Dad, what else can we do to help sell these golf balls? How do we get people to stop?"

I told him to always smile and to ask passers-by if they wanted to buy some golf balls. I also coached him on asking people how their day was and how their golf was going.

I watched as the next golf cart drove up. By now, Joshua had shared these strategies with Joel and John (their little brother who was now interested in this developing situation). So when the next golf cart arrived, Joshua, Joel, and John had a huge smile on their faces. That got the cart to stop. Then I heard them ask, "Would you like to buy some golf balls?

That was it. First sale. $5!

There's nothing like that first cash coming into your business. The boys sprinted over to me, bouncing around, excited, totally pumped up. "Dad, Dad, Dad. We just made five dollars!"

This went on the rest of the day. They adapted their questions to get a higher closing ratio (the percentage of people who bought) on the golfers. They also quickly identified the prime buyers of golf balls.

As they started to get sales, they began to focus on who was buying. This is a critical step to creating any winning offer. Identify your buyers and focus your efforts on them (the boys were getting demographics).

This is an important marketing lesson. You must know who your buyer is. What is the demographic? What do they like? Why do they buy?

Once you know this, then you speak to that audience. What do they want to hear? How do they talk? We've said this before, but you need to know who is buying what you are selling. And then tailor your message to their needs.

You might be able to guess who the best demographic/ clients were for my boys. It was pretty obvious early on. Grandmas were money in the bank! How can a Grandma refuse three cute boys? They couldn't say no to three ambitious boys selling a product they really needed at a great price point!

This is an irresistible offer—specifically catered to this market!

The closing ratio went through the roof with Grandmas! Soon the boys only ran over to sell balls for Grandmas. The rest of the time they would just play in the background and watch the men and younger women pass by. They knew they could work a lot less and get huge results. (They were learning the power of focus and doing the highest leverage activity! Even a 6-year-old can do this. Or John, the 2-year-old.)

5. Thank Your Customer

The next task we identified was to thank their customers. The boys were so excited from the first few sales that they did not express their appreciation. But I soon said to them. "You guys are doing great. You are starting to get sales. You are getting bigger sales. Now we must figure out how to get more frequency to your sales."

How could they get buyers to buy more often and take advantage of word-of-mouth advertising?

Part of the answer was to make a huge first impression. We didn't want to just thank them. We needed to do something the customers would remember, to do something that might even get us referral sales.

We came up with the idea to give everyone a thank you card with some information about us. The boys spent the next day taking colored paper and crayons and writing a simple message. They colored the cards and drew happy kids (themselves) smiling from ear to ear, saying "Thank you for buying golf balls."

A simple message. A simple gesture. But a powerful impact. Simplicity often makes the biggest impact.

It wasn't long until any golfer we bumped into (and some who didn't golf) would mention how amazing our kids were. Our kids were "branding" themselves. Word was spreading. Business was growing.

The only problem was it was late fall and winter was approaching. So for now it was a seasonal business, but I was sure my kids would figure out a way to increase business among their existing clients. We'd have to wait and see!

To recap, here are the steps we took to create a winning offer (step 2 of the Reverse Online Profits™ system):

- Discover what people want to buy

- Find a solution

- Create an irresistible offer

- Take action, adjust, adapt

- Thank your customer

These are the five critical parts of creating a winning offer and setting yourself up for success in step No. 2 of the Reverse Online Profits™ system.

Here's a picture of my kids and their winning offer.

This is a pretty basic marketing and business plan. It is simple. The boys took action and got a result. Action creates results. Even with the simplest ideas, if you put action behind them you will get results.

The best plan with little action will yield no results. So take action now. Develop some new skill sets. Don't make it harder than it really is. Get a plan and take action.

Creating a powerful, irresistible offer is so easy that even a 6-year-old can do it! So can you! The story about my sons' business is a great example of creating an offer offline or online.

Next, let's tie this all together with an example of how

to create an irresistible offer for a potential client, from the start of that client's experience till the first sale is made or desired action is taken with your company. We will cover the entire process from the advertisement to your desired result. There are a few specific items you must do since you are going to be building your business online. Let's get to it.

A Winning Offer from A to Z Online

When you follow the Reverse Online Profits™ (ROP) system, you will always focus first on finding the money-making website. After you find a website, use the Green Light System. Next, you will have to create your offer, the marketing funnel. This is step 2 in the ROP system.

Here's a typical marketing funnel or process on the Internet:

- A person clicks on your ad (search, Facebook, banner, etc.).

- The person who clicked on your ad arrives at your website.

- That person reviews your website and decides to stay or leave (all within about three to five seconds or less).

- If the person stays, they will engage with your website, possibly by giving you some of their information (they might become a part of your email list).

- You will lead the person through more information to help them make a buying decision.

- Once a sale is made, you offer other products and services to increase the initial value of the transaction or to raise the frequency of transactions.

- The person arrives at a "thank you page."

This is a general overview of any marketing funnel online. Let's walk through some of these steps to help you create the most effective, cash-creating marketing funnels.

It all starts with the ad.

Ad Creation

If there is one word that best describes this entire process, it has got to be congruency. It is not just about having one working part of your offer, but it's about having every step flow from the previous step. You must be consistent with your marketing efforts and what you offer people who are just waiting to give money to you.

This first step is critical. In fact, it sets the tone for the rest of the experience you create for the person coming into your marketing funnel.

We will focus on three main parts of an ad for now:

- Headline

- Image

- Call to action

The most important part of your ad is your headline.

1. Create and Test Headlines

This is the first step. When you are making an ad, you have to test your headline. In the Internet world, it is the headline that makes or breaks your ad, because it is the first thing that your customers see. If I go and type "lose 10 lbs in 3 days" in Google, and I find an ad that says exactly the same thing, do you think I would click on that ad and look at what it has to say? Yes.

If the headline says what your customers want to see or hear, then your results will be better. The key here is to test many headlines. Test every step of this process, but especially this first step. What you learn with your ad headline can help predict what will work best through your entire buying funnel. This is why headlines are important, and testing your headlines is important, because it is only through testing that you know what really works.

Of course you can simply assume that a particular headline will work, but you will never really know for sure unless you test it, so don't be lazy. The way to test a headline is simply to let it run and see how many people click on it. The stronger the headline, the more clicks it will receive. More importantly, the stronger the headline, the more products people actually buy.

Tips for Writing Killer Headlines

I have a few tips that you can use when it comes to constructing click-inducing headlines.

First, if you are doing an ad within a search engine, be sure to put your keywords in your headlines. If the keyword that you are targeting is "how to train dogs," make sure that it is in your headline. Say something like, "Free: How To Train Dogs In 7 Days." If the keyword that you are targeting is weight loss, make sure your ad has those exact words to catch the attention of potential customers.

When you have an ad that gets clicked more than the other ads, you will pay less for the clicks than your competitors. I'll talk about the importance of Click Through Rates (CTR) on an ad later and how it affects how much money you pay to get a click to your website. For now, just realize that writing good headlines heavily affects your CTR, which in turn can lower your advertising cost.

Obviously, the biggest things on your website that people see are headlines, so you have to get their attention immediately. What works best? Headlines should address their most pressing needs (related to the topic) immediately.

If people are looking for ways to train their dog, the headline should be all about solving their problems in training their dogs. If they are looking for their pizza to be delivered on time, the headline should be all about delivering their pizza on time. Keep it simple. Don't over-think the process.

Another great strategy is to see which headlines work best and then incorporate those headlines into your website. If a headline gets more clicks and buyers on a search engine, chances are it will also get more clicks and buyers on your website. For example, if you want to test headlines, you can run ads with the headlines you want to use and see which headline converts the most! It saves you a massive headache before building your website.

Let's look at an example on Google. Let's search for "Key Largo real estate."

Notice the first ad matches the keywords I typed in. In fact, the words in the top two ads are exactly like those I typed in. Which one of the ads do you think would be the one you would click on? You would probably be like me and click on something that is exactly what you typed in. That's how we work. We search for something and when we see it, we click on it.

If you clicked on the ad, what do you think would be the best words to see on the page that comes up?

You would want it to say something congruent with what you just typed. So if the page said "Key Largo real estate" on the top, you would feel the most "at home." You would think this is where you should be.

However, when I clicked on the top two websites, I didn't see the words "Key Largo real estate" anywhere. That's a bummer. If they would have told me immediately what I was looking for, I'd hang out on their site longer. Be sure to use the keywords on the first page of your website as often as you can. Also, use a visual of the words that people typed in Google on your website. More on that in a minute.

Also note that if you don't have your own website, but are acting as an affiliate for another site, you want to build ads with headlines that match the affiliate website headlines for maximum results!

Remember, be congruent. It starts with the headline, so keep them going on the same message for maximum conversions, results, and dollars.

2. Use Images to Shape Minds

Images are critical. Sometimes you can have a pretty bad headline, but if your image gets people's attention, you can still make money. Always test images, whether in a Facebook ad, banner ad, or on your website. If you are building a website, there are certain images, colors, and other strategies that work best for certain demographics. Also, you can add an image that matches the search words/terms people use in search engines. This is in addition to having those words on the first page of your website, as we pointed out before, so that your visitors can see them when they click on the ad words.

For example, for our "Key Largo real estate" search, the website could have had a picture of a map with Key Largo and some beautiful houses. Did you notice how Google showed a map of Key Largo in their search results? Do you think this is by accident? Or do you think the company may have tested what makes people feel best served so that people think they are on the right page? Google spends a lot of money on testing such things, so learn from them.

By the way, we are talking about demographics. Demographics simply are about identifying who is coming to your website: young, old, male, female, black, white, American, Australian, holding a college degree, holding a high school degree, etc. You will use demographics when creating ads or targeting ads on certain websites where you want to draw traffic from.

If you don't know the demographics, you can take the website you found in step 1 and simply plug it into a paid version of Compete.com or go to Google.com/adplanner, Quantcast.com, or Alexa.com. These websites will all show you who is on a site. I like to use Google.com/adplanner. It's free and will give you details on who is on a website and what other websites those people visit. (I also use this tool in step 1 when we are finding a money website. You get some great information here.)

Let's use the Monster.com job search site as an example on Google.com/adplanner.

Using Google ad planner, we can get an idea of the demographics of the people visiting Monster.com. They are 62 percent female and mostly in the 35-54 age group. Almost 90 percent of the visitors have a college degree or some education, with average household income in the $25,000-$50,000 range.

So if you are Monster.com and you are creating ads on your website, you want to cater to the majority of visitors: women, 35-54, with some education and an income of $25,000-$50,000. That's a lot of information.

The Monster.com website color is purple. Why do you think that is? I'd say it matches the site's demographic.

Let's research this a little. I just went to Google and typed in "what does purple symbolize?" The top site listed is color-wheel-pro.com/color-meaning.html. About the color purple, it says:

Light purple is a good choice for a feminine design.

Dark purple evokes gloom and sad feelings. It can cause frustration.

Monster.com is dark purple. The demographics show us the majority of the users are women. So purple fits this demographic. Also, many people in between jobs or in jobs they hate may feel frustrated or sad. So Monster's use of purple would also relate to anyone feeling this way who is looking for a job.

When you start to learn why websites, TV, politicians, and others say what they say, it will start to blow you away. It's all marketing. It's all about telling the audience what makes them feel like they are in the right place. It's really pretty amazing. You don't have to dive this deep into everything you do, but if you are building a brand and business I would invest the time to get your demographic information down, because it will affect not only your headlines, but everything you do.

We can apply the use of demographics to the creation of ads and also to creating your website. More on that in a moment.

3. Have a Call to Action

When you create an advertisement, you can also add one more important element to it: a call to action. This is where you tell the person what to do. In a banner ad, this may simply say "click here for _____" or something like that. If you are writing a Facebook ad or search ad, you can add some words after your headline to direct the user to take an action. For example, if we have a headline of "Free Dog Training Video," we might include, "in 30 seconds, Free Video Reveals the #1 Mistake Most Dog Owners make— Find out Now" or something like that. Calls to action are cool, because, as we have talked about earlier, you always have to pre-sell the next click—meaning warm them up to the next action—because that is what ultimately makes you money.

Adding numbers to your PPC (pay-per-click) ads are gold, too, because people like numbers. For example, you can say "7 secret dog training tricks revealed" or "5 mistakes dog owners make in training their dogs" or stuff like that. Using numbers works well.

Now you need to start creating ads. Get a piece of paper and start taking notes. Go to where you are going to advertise. Look at what others are doing that is working (like the ROP system teaches) and start to come up with your own ideas. Write out twenty different headlines to test. Pick the best ten and start testing. You will have to pay for those ads to test the headlines, but the answers will be well worth the investment.

Create the Website

After you worked hard to get people to your website, then what? We've already mentioned the critical concept and key to any click. Pre-sell it; then take the visitor to a page where the user feels "at home." You don't want people to click and come to your site and say, "What the heck is this?" You must be congruent with what you are offering — the ad should be similar to what you are offering on the landing page (the first page a person sees after clicking on an ad). If you start with dog training on the ad, your website must be about dog training, too.

Remember the importance of demographics when creating an ad. Let's look at how to use this information to create a website that appeals to your new visitor. For example, if you are trying to capture dog owners, you might want to put a photo of a dog on your website. If you are trying to capture women who are looking for weight loss, you might want to decide what demographics of women you want to target and put up a photo on the site that matches what they want. You rarely see images of overweight people on weight-loss websites. Weight-loss websites usually show smiling, happy people. There is a reason. This is what the person visiting this site wants to be.

For specifics in your marketing, you may be able to get a lot of information from your competitor's website. Look at the photos on the website and then go to Google's Ad planner to check out the demographics of the traffic they are receiving. Chances are, if the website of your competitor is any good, the photo on their website is the exact image of what their target visitors are looking for.

You can also test your images. For example, if you are trying to test images for the dog-training niche, you can try to put an image of a golden retriever on one ad and maybe a Chihuahua on the other, and see which ad makes more conversions—that is, which ad has more people actually buying products from the site. If you are targeting golden retriever owners, use a picture of a golden retriever on your website. For all you know, there are people out there who would want trained Chihuahuas more than trained golden retrievers! So just test your images; particularly when you are running Facebook ads, images are gold.

Congruency Is Key

Don't forget to make everything relevant to your key-word, make everything congruent. For example, let's say you're fifty pounds overweight and are looking for a weight-loss guide. You might type in the search term "weight loss" on Google.com. Which domain would you click on? The ad that says lose24pounds.com or the ad that says lose-50pounds.com? Remember, congruency is key— and people want to see what they are looking for. It is that simple.

Follow the First-Glance Rule

One of the most powerful rules that you can follow in website creation is called the first-glance rule. It pretty much sums up how people make decisions: they are based on first impressions.

You should create every webpage, every ad, and every step with one goal in mind. That should be the focus of that page. Anything that interferes with this action should be removed. Anything and everything that you have going on in that website should contribute to the realization of that goal.

Let me repeat. One action per step. Remove everything else, or you will confuse people. Don't give them choices. Point the way for the user to go.

If your website does not meet that goal or does not motivate people to reach that goal, your website will not work.

Be Sure to Test

This also highlights the importance of testing. When creating a website, you should create several templates and see which one converts more. For example, you can have the same website in three different colors or designs. It will not take long before you see differences in click-through rates and conversions. Always test one variable at a time.

Let me give you an example. Have you ever noticed how many shopping carts (on the "buy" button) on different websites are colored yellow/orange? That is because tests have shown that the yellow/orange color converts more visitors! I like to keep my eyes on Amazon.com, one of the top retailing sites on the Internet. The company tests everything. And it sells billions and billions each year on its website. It invests heavily into testing which clicks convert best.

The smallest change to increase conversions can increase sales by hundreds of millions of dollars. This is a great website to study continuously. Have you noticed which color all its "call to action" buttons are? Yup, mainly orange with black words and an outline. You'd be wise to test this on your website.

Set up the Landing Page

The first page people see after clicking on an ad is often called a "landing page." It's the page they first arrive at on your website. They have all ears and eyes on you! But, only for about three seconds. Then, in most cases, they'll be gone, unless you can figure out ways to keep them on the page.

Here are some pointers on how to create high-converting websites/landing pages after someone clicks on your ad:

1. Have the keyword of what they were searching for on the page (if they come through search).

2. Have an image on the page to match the needs of the person arriving there (for search or banner).

3. Images on the left side are great for capturing a person's attention. Remember that people in the U.S. read from left to right, so when they come to your website they will start looking at the left side of the page and quickly move right. Your goal is to have a headline and an image on the left to keep them on your site.

4. Have a killer headline on top of the page to the right of the image (visitors' eyes will go from image to headline).

5. Put your call to action on the right side of the page

6. Put your call to action above the fold of the page (meaning they don't have to browse down your site to find out what you want them to do.)

7. Use images to attract eyes on the page to the desired message.

8. Shut up! What I mean is you don't usually need to give a lot of information to get a desired action if the above elements are working. Keep words to a minimum.

9. Use color variation to direct eyes from the left to the right.

10. Put a picture of what they might get on the call to action buttons.

11. Take away fear of the action.

To illustrate some of these points, let's look at an example of a landing page—it's for the website we are using to market the book you are reading right now.

Take note of a few elements on this page:

1. The main keyword is "Internet Millionaire" and/or "Jeff Usner." Both are the main focus of this page.

2. We use a strong visual of the book (you know what you are getting).

3. The visual is on the left side of the page.

4. The headline is "Get a copy of Jeff Usner's Internet Millionaire" (this is the reason why visitors came to this page from an email or banner ad).

5. We tell them what to do: "Enter Your Name and Email to Get Your Book" (call to action) on the right side of page.

6. We "lead" eyes to the green button. We use a green button on this step to "get book." We will test this versus the yellow/orange buy button, but we aren't asking people to buy yet on this page. Green means go, and we use this color on many pages where people aren't buying yet.

7. The call to action "Get Book" is above the fold so you don't have to browse down the page.

8. We shut up! We don't discuss anything else on this page, only the main action we want them to take.

After the visitors fill out the "Get the Book" page, they are taken to another page where there is a video (not shown) describing what they will get. Take a look at a call to action button from an order page below.

You'll notice the following on the call to action for someone buying this book:

- The color of the button is close to the Amazon.com button.

- We show 100% satisfaction guaranteed.

- We show the book cover.

- We show we accept Visa/MasterCard (they know they can buy).

Here's the next page people see after clicking on "Add To Cart." At this step, buyers see:

- Picture of book again.

- An order process on top bar; they are in the "registration" step.

- We carried their name and email from the last page (they feel familiar with the page).

- We have client testimonials on the page (shows proof others like our products too!).

- We use the words "Continue Your Order Below" (again, letting them know they are on the right page; they are simply "continuing" through this process).

Remember to use the ROP System.

Remember, don't try to reinvent the wheel. Study what your competitors are doing. Check out their website and see what it is all about. Ask yourself:

- What do you like about their website?

- What do you hate about their website?

- What improvements can you do?

- If you are a potential customer, how would you react to seeing that kind of website?

Here are some other parts of a marketing campaign you should test in your offer:

- Website colors

- Price

- Guarantee

- Headlines

- Credit card (payment plans)

- Rebilling ability

- How is product delivered? Digital, hard copy?

Study Similar Websites

Again, to make sure that you are doing this properly, and by properly I mean the best money-making way, all you have to do is look at similar websites offering the same thing and doing the same thing and see how they do it. This is practically the best way to see all the strategies and techniques that are making money. It is not guesswork, because you can use the tools that I mentioned earlier to see hard stats on how well these other websites perform and make money. All you have to do now is replicate it yourself.

If you have found a money-making website offering what you are looking to offer, buy its product and return it to see how it handles returns. See what it's bringing to the table and improve on that and just crush it.

Once you go in there and do it, you'd really be surprised how simple it can be.

Get Inside Prospects' Heads

Just remember that to make the most conversions from your ad, email, or offer, you must get inside the head of your prospects!

You have to approach the creation of your offer from the shoes of your prospects and not from the point of view of an Internet marketer. The offer you create must be benefit-laden, something that your target customers want and need. You must get in their mind set and think like they think.

Why do they have this problem? What would it mean to them to have the problem solved? What do they like about the solution? How will it make them feel? Ask yourself questions and pretend to be your client.

You don't want to talk about a long list of features on your website or offer. Bottom line, people don't care about features. They care about what your product or service will do for them. How will it help them? How will it make them feel? If you wrap your offer in such a way that it solves their pains, takes care of their most urgent problems, and lays out the solution for them to go get, you will have a winning offer.

Make a Promise You Can Keep

Make a bold promise in your offer, something that they are looking for, and something that you can positively deliver. For example, you can say that your product can solve their problems in seven days and if it doesn't, buyers get their money back 100 percent, no questions asked! That's a bold statement. It solves my problem and takes away my fear of losing money. If it doesn't work, I get my money back. That's a bold statement. It is all a matter of figuring out what you can promise to your clients and being bold about promising and delivering on this promise.

Use Success Stories

Provide proof of success to support your assertions. This is important, because you want customers to trust you, so always give them proof by sharing stories—success stories—on how your offer has fulfilled your promise for other satisfied customers. This is one of the most critical pieces to your marketing. Share stories of people's results. Focus on sharing results. I learned a statement a long time ago that goes like this: Facts tell, stories sell.

As you create your winning offer, take time to ask your customers for feedback. If you don't have any clients yet, you can start without stories, but as soon as you get clients, ask them to share their success. Then publish their success wherever you can.

Get Strategic with Domain Names

1. Similar domain with www.www-domain.com strategy:

Let's say you are targeting the keyword "dog training" but there is already an existing domain with that keyword, like dogtraining.com or dogtraining.net or dogtraining. whatever. Do you settle for other keywords instantly? Well, no, not exactly. You should try the arrow technique, which is actually pretty cool. Most Internet marketers do not know about it.

This strategy is simple, but effective. If you can't get the domain you want, you may be able to get something close to it. You could get a domain that looks like this: www.www-dogtraining.com in the event that www.dogtraining.com is already owned by someone else.

The best thing about it is that your site appears as the keyword that you are targeting without having any hassle at all. You can remove the first www part by not adding it to your display url, so when people search for dog training on search engines, your site will appear to them as www-dogtraining.com. You get a domain which could give you a much higher click through rate and, as a result, lower your cost per click.

2. Short urls are also great:

You want to use domains with less than 14 to 16 characters if possible. You don't want to look like www.howtotrainyourdogsandhousebreakthem.com, because, for one, search engines will not allow that and, frankly, that name is hard to read. The best strategy is to find some domain with less characters. Get a domain people can read quickly, and pronounce and spell easily.

3. Buy misspellings:

Another great thing about domains is misspellings. There is a lot of money to be made from misspellings. Be sure to buy any misspellings of your domain.

I learned about misspellings the hard way when I owned a website called GreatLegalLeads.com. It was a good name for our business/website at that time. We were selling leads of people looking for legal help. One day, I got an email from someone who said they didn't like our leads. When I followed up with the person, I discovered something shocking.

This person had been typing in "greatlegaleads.com." Do you see the difference? There is only one "l" in the domain name between "legal" and "leads." This person hadn't even been buying leads from our company. Other people were misspelling our domain, too, and were going to a competitor's website. At first, I was a little ticked off at the competitor. Then I realized this was fair game, and I should have owned the other domain. There are people who make a lot of money doing this. They might simply redirect to a website with ads on it and make money selling ads or using Google AdSense on a new site they create. So remember to buy your misspelled domain names.

Now that you have found and made your own money-making website/business, let's move on to the next step where you will learn how to get the most qualified people to your website. After all, you can have the best offer in the world, but without traffic, you won't sell a thing. You won't have that problem after this next chapter. Your challenge might be how to fill all the orders you have!

CHAPTER 5

Get People To Your Website

Traffic? Who Likes Traffic?

Let's picture your business as a lake. It's where your offer is, it's where your people are, it's the heart of all you do. What feeds the lake? Rivers, streams, and creeks. Without these, most lakes will dry up. Now, let's imagine two pictures of rivers feeding the lake (your business).

The first is a dried-up river with everything around and in it dead. Nothing is thriving, living, or growing. Nothing is moving; nothing is happening. There is no momentum. Every once in a while there will be a rainstorm and the river kicks up a little bit, but it quickly dies back down. It's famine time when no river is flowing, leading to a dried-up lake. The lake is also barren, and no fruit is seen anywhere. Hopeless, dead.

You can look at where the river should be flowing. It might be flowing by some of the best lands in the world, but without water, that land also is dead and useless. The land bears no fruit. It has no effect on anyone. It's not feeding anyone; it's not creating jobs for people, and it's ugly and dead. That's it.

Now let's look at the opposite scenario. Let's look at a flowing, gushing, raging, overpowering river with life thriving in and around it. The fields beside this river are erupting with vegetation. A powerful raging river is hard to stop. It's a hard place to get out of once you are in it. It's one of the most magnificent scenes when you see an unstoppable, unbeatable river pounding through a mountainside. The lake receiving the water is also overflowing, supplying the vital needs of the countryside.

Which lake would you like your business to look like?

I've experienced both. The first dried-up river, with nothing flowing into your business, leads to debt, failure, stress, laying off people, and unhappy clients, employees, owners, spouses, etc. The smallest challenges seem ever so large when there is little or no traffic.

When your business has one, two, three, or more gushing rivers fueling its growth, it's lights on. Profits are flowing, people are happy, the momentum is unstoppable, you are unbeatable, and challenges seem minor, because so much good is going on.

With your online business, traffic from visitors is like water from streams and rivers filling a lake. Mastering the skill set of driving online traffic is—as far I can tell—one of the highest-paid professions in the world. When you can learn to bring the most high quality people in the front of any business, you become unstoppable. You get the freedom to do this for your own business or by simply setting up streams of traffic to other websites and collecting checks; sometimes those checks flow to you for years after setting up traffic just one time.

Let's review where you are right now in the Reverse Online Profits™ system. You've completed finding a money market/website.

We've covered replicating and creating a winning offer. Now you are in step 3: replicate traffic.

This is a critical step in the process. If you have a winning website/offer/product/service, that's great. But if no one is coming to your website, you will go out of business.

These next two chapters cover some of my favorite activities—replicating and creating traffic. This is where I invest a lot of time. I love it. It's great for helping others scale their businesses and take any business to a new level. And in my experience, I've discovered and uncovered some sizzling hot business secrets.

After this chapter, you will know more about traffic than 99 percent of the people on the Internet. I'll show you how to buy up all the media you can handle for up to 50 percent or less than what your competitors pay in order to drive traffic to your website. You will also learn how to find the keywords, websites, and ads, which make all the money you need so you don't have to ever buy cash-sucking traffic.

Before we get into where you can get traffic to your website, there are few methods we will cover at the end of the chapter where you can almost "copy and paste" the exact keywords or demographics to get the highest qualified traffic. This is literally what we do almost every day in our office. Again, we don't try to reinvent the wheel, but we simply use tools like Compete.com, Wordtracker.com, and KeywordSpy.com to get the right keywords and demographics to bid on. I love copy and paste. It's a system made simple for you.

In many cases, we literally launch a new campaign by simply doing copy and paste.

Generate Traffic

There are several areas where you can get traffic. Here's a brief overview:

There are three main areas of traffic we'll cover in this chapter. Keep in mind as we work through this chapter that this is an introduction to traffic. I will attempt to make it as easy as possible for newbies and include some gold nuggets for the professionals reading this.

Here are the three areas:

- Pay-per-click search engines

- Facebook ads

- Media buying

Each one of these traffic sources is explosive and has the potential to deliver you enough highly qualified people to double, triple, or quadruple any business.

Search Engine Marketing

Let's go back to a story I shared in Chapter 1. When I was discussing how newbies get crushed, I had talked about the weight-loss product I promoted that made me almost $7,000 on my first day. One thing I did not reveal is that most of this traffic came from just one keyword. To be more exact, the traffic came from the exact match of a keyword. This exact-match keyword earned more than $20,000 that first week, all from one keyword. I will define the term "exact match" later.

First, you need to understand how search engines like Google, Yahoo, Bing, and others work. How do you get your listing to No. 1 on the sites without having to take time developing and building links to your website, etc.?

Here's an example, using the keyword phrase "how to find a real estate agent." This is the picture of a search on Google:

You will notice that the tan listing on the top and the listings on the far right (under the label "Why these ads?") are all ads. This is paid advertising.

The sites appearing below the tan box are called "organic listings." These are free listings. They are free in that you don't have to pay Google to get the position on the search results page. You employ something called Search Engine Optimization (SEO) to get listed higher in those listings. We won't discuss SEO in this book, because it's a broad, intensive, ever-changing strategy to build traffic.

We are going to focus on the paid listings. You will see that Yahoo.com has a similar set-up when you go to the site and do a search. The more ads you see around the subject of your interest, the more money is being spent on the niche, which is cool, because the marketers would not be advertising there and spending their hard-earned cash if they were not making money on the topic. It's pretty basic, right? You spend money advertising on something that makes you even more money.

Now you know what we are talking about. Where your ad shows up is dependent on a few factors. Here are the main factors determining where you show up on the paid listings.

1. **Bid price:** This is simply the "bid" you make on a keyword to determine how much you would pay per click.

2. **CTR:** Stands for click through rate. This is the percentage of how many times a person clicks on your ad versus another ad or listing.

3. **Landing page relevancy to keyword:** Google, Yahoo, and others will take a "quick peek" at your website to determine if your website has anything to do with the keyword you are bidding on and give you a "quality score" based on this inspection.

These are the three main factors determining how much you pay and where you show up on the search results on these search engines. We will explore these three factors later in this chapter, and I'll share with you how you can manipulate these factors to pay as little as 50 percent or less than your competitors. There are some other factors, too, but if we focus on the three, we can beat out 90 percent of the competition.

Next, let's define a few more terms you need to know when dominating search engine traffic. There are four phrases to describe the type of bids you make to buy clicks on search engines.

1. Exact match

2. Phrase match

3. Broad match

4. Negative keywords

1. Exact Match

This is when you have picked a keyword and you only bid on the exact match of that keyword. For example, if I were to bid on the term "How to lose 10 pounds in 30 days," I could set it up so my ad showed up only when all of those words appeared in that exact sequence, with no other words before or after the phrase. My ad only shows up when the keyword phrase someone is searching for on Google exactly matches the term I am bidding on.

2. Phrase Match

Let's look at the term "how to lose 10 pounds in 30 days" in the example above. For the exact match bid, your ad would only show up if people typed in all of those words—

nothing more, nothing less. However, in a phrase match, your ad would display to those using just a phrase, even with words in the front or back, of what you bid on. So for the term above, if you bid on the phrase match of "lose 10 pounds," your ad would potentially show up in searches for the following phrases:

- "how to lose 10 pounds'"
- "Lose 10 pounds in 30 days"
- "How to Lose 10 pounds in 40 days"
- "I want to learn how to Lose 10 pounds in 10 days"
- "lose 10 pounds in winter"

In each of these search phrases, the words "lose 10 pounds" are together within a larger phrase, so your ad would potentially show up for all these searches.

In order for your ad to show up on a phrase match, the phrase you bid on has to be in the same order within another search. Your ad wouldn't show up for "lose 8 to 10 pounds in 10 days," because the statement doesn't include your core phrase in the order you wanted. It's similar but does not include the entire phrase in order.

3. Broad phrase

This is when you bid on any phrase as long as it has your keyword. So if you bid on "10 pounds" with a broad phrase, your ad could potentially show up in the following searches:

- "lose 10 pounds"
- "buy 10 pounds of steaks"

- "10 pounds of chocolate"
- "I like 10 slices of pound cake"

With this type of phrase matching, your ad will show up for many phrases that have nothing to do with what you are actually getting traffic for. We rarely bid on broad phrase traffic unless we are doing another advanced strategy, which I will share later, focused on "demographic" bidding of words.

In that case, we have a high converting offer on a broad audience in which, if we just get the demographic of people clicking on our ads, we can make money. This is when you view search engines more like a media buy or Facebook ad, when you bid on terms a certain demographic might bid on. Again, this is very advanced, and I'll go through it later.

4. Negative keywords

This is when you include words you don't want your ad to appear for.

In our previous example on the broad match for "10 pounds," if we didn't want our ad to show up for "10 pounds of chocolate," we could include the word "chocolate" as a word we don't want our ad to show up with.

If we did this, our ad wouldn't show to those searching for the phrase "10 pounds of chocolate," for example.

This may seem like a lot of information, but at this point, just think of it as learning a new language. In any new profession, you need to learn new words, phrases, and terms. When I started a job at an Olive Garden restaurant back the 1990s, I went through a week of training to learn its language. This industry is no different.

The good news is I am going to show you a way to cut out 90 percent of the learning curve and simply bid on words that make money.

To set up a search campaign on Google, go to Google. com/adwords. To set up a campaign on Yahoo or Bing, go to adcenter.microsoft.com.

Here are the basic steps to get started on search marketing:

1. Create campaign

2. Create ad group

3. Created ad

4. Choose keywords

Let's go through each step with some money-making pointers to help you get more traffic for less money.

1. Create Campaign

Each platform is a little different, but the good news is Google and Adcenter have invested a lot of money to make it as easy as possible for you to set up your first campaign. Why? They want you to succeed and give them more money!

Here are two points for creating a new campaign:

- Set up a daily budget (keep it low to start — we'll discuss this more in depth shortly).

- Set up the area where you want your ad to run. Where do you want your ad to run: United States, Canada, India, Texas, or Beverly Hills? You decide.

Please be sure to do this with any campaign you set up. We have this on our checklists at our office, because I have made mistakes in the past that cost us thousands of dollars before we figured out what was going on—our budget was not set low to start.

2. Create Ad Group

The second step is to click on the words "Create Ad Group" to create an ad group that is very relevant to your campaign. So if you are creating a campaign on used cars in Google, your ad groups may be broken down by types of cars. You might have an ad group for Honda, Volkswagen, Ford, Chevy, and so on. This will help with your overall performance in your campaigns and ad groups, and ultimately help to lower your costs.

3. Create Ad

The key with ads goes back to the strategies discussed in the last chapter, where you needed to write an ad for your audience. You have to write ads that people would want to click on. You don't always know what will work, so I suggest you test at least three to five different ads.

The slight difference in ads can increase click-throughs and lower your click costs by up to 50 percent or more. Remember, congruency is key. Think about the "how to find a real estate agent" ad. The ad with the headline and copy that was close to my search would probably get the most clicks.

Here are ways to create powerful ads:

1. Test headlines: Run three to five different ads to start. Look at competitors' ads to get a good idea of what is already working and base your ads on those. This will take the guesswork out of ad creation and you don't have to become a master copywriter. If you find an ad that has been on Google for months, believe me, it's

working. Once you start to get traffic from your test headlines, it will not take long to see who the winner is.

Part of what you should test is using your keyword in the headline. Sometimes this works well, and other times it doesn't. For example, you can set up your ads so that Google or Adcenter will display the keyword the users typed into their search engine. Google and Adcenter will automatically put the keyword a user types into your ad. If you do this, many times you will get the highest CTR (click through rate), but the clicks coming through may not be of the best quality, unless you match that word on your next page a hundred percent (which you can do — I'll show a secret ninja trick we use to do this).

But beware, high CTRs are not always what you want. If the click doesn't convert to a sale or action on your website, then it is not the best thing to do. So testing is most important. Test at least three ads to begin with. For example, if you are selling picture frames, you might use a headline "Free Picture Frame." This ad would get a lot of clicks. But maybe what you meant or what you actually say on your website is "Free picture frame with the purchase of $50 or more." If you don't mention this in the ad, visitors arriving at your website may not want to spend money, so you might get a lot of clicks but low conversions.

2. Use a domain in the ad that includes the keyword: This is not always possible, but once you know your "dominant keyword," you can create a domain with that word or words in the domain. You might also want to

get different domains for different campaigns. Again, this takes time, but if you find a keyword or group of keywords that make you a lot of money, it's worth the time to get a domain that matches the money-making words and build a site around that keyword.

Remember, if you do this right, you can set this up one time and profit from it for years. For example, if you have a business selling designer cowboy boots, you would want to get a domain as close as possible to "designercowboyboots.com" if this was the No. 1 keyword that brought buyers to your website. If the keyword matches the website, then a user doing the search will regard your website more highly, because if that's your name, you must be good at what you are called! This is what a user thinks.

3. Use the arrow technique when you can: This technique is really simple and effective, but most Internet marketers do not use it at all! The arrow technique takes advantage of the way people read online, because most of the time when people see an ad they do not even read it! They just scan it.   Therefore, you want to use the arrow technique so when they scan your ad, it results in them buying, and making money for you.

How to Use the Arrow Technique

Usually when you write your ad, it follows this template:

HEADLINE
Subheadline 1
Subheadline 2
DOMAIN

Like this:

> **Free Music Downloads**
> The Safest and Most Valid Way to
> **Download Free Music! Download**
> **Now.**
> iMesh.com

With the arrow technique, you structure your ad this way:

KEYWORD
KEYWORD. Text. Text. Text.
Text. Text. Text. KEYWORD.
KEYWORD in the domain.

So the above ad could read like this on a search for "free music":

Free Music Downloads
100's of Songs: **Free Music**
Free Music Within 30 Seconds.
iMesh.com/FreeMusic

Let me tell you why this works. People naturally read from left to right, so when they see your keywords in strategic places, like in the upper left part of the text, magic happens, because that is where the English-reading eye goes first when reading. People see your keyword first and "feel at home." It's like your ad is the one thing that they have been waiting for all their life to change their fate and lead them to happily ever after! It's crazy!

Also remember that when you type a keyword in a search engine, the words that match on the ad get bolded, so you know that the arrow technique is a serious killer, because your arrow is now bold and even more visible for a searcher to find you. Instant attention, more impact, and more money for you.

- Using the www-domain technique: Ideally, you want to get a domain with the keyword on your url right, but if the keyword that you want is already purchased by your competitor or someone else, the way to get a killer domain is to do the www-technique. Your domain will look like this www.www-keyword.com and when you pick your display url, all you do is omit the first "www" part so your domain shows up like www-keyword.com. It is a pretty cool tactic that you should consider.

- Use short urls: You do this because they are optimized best and help your target audience find you. Good urls, such as movies.com, are short and highly related to your niche or focused on keywords. Bad urls, such as those with four more words strung together, are not as relevant and harder for visitors to find.

- Use numbers in ads: In copywriting and testing thousands of ads, I've found that numbers in ads almost always outperform ads without numbers. Numbers in headlines like "7 Secrets to X" or "5 Worst of That" work well. In the earlier example, note that in the second ad, I used "100's of Songs" in the first subheadline. I would bet this would outperform the ad we see above without the number.

- Create urgency in ads. In the above example ad, I also added an element of speed/delivery when I said "within 30 seconds." When people are doing a search, they want to find their answers as quickly as possible. So I basically told them, "Hey, within 30 seconds you will have what you want." This can drive up your CTR on any advertisement. You have to make sure you can back up the ad and actually deliver on the promise you make. It wouldn't need to be 30 seconds if you can't deliver in 30 seconds. If it took your website three minutes, you should test ads using the words "within 3 minutes."

- Capitalize each word in a PPC (pay per click) ad: If you look at the earlier example, you will see that all the primary words in the ad are capitalized. This works 99 percent of the time. I don't know why, but it draws in visitors. You can also use this in Facebook ads, but the site will limit the number of capitalized words, so choose the words you want to emphasize wisely.

- Use ", [, {, or any type of non-numerical symbol or letter in the front of your ad. You might have a headline say "3 Ways" to Get Free Music" and use the "" (quotation marks) around your ad. It's just another thing to draw users' eyes to your ads and get you clicks.

- We will cover ramping and banking in a later chapter, which will show you how Google and Adcenter give you a free tool to determine exactly what your keywords are making, so you can adjust each one to make it profitable (or to pause). This has simplified the process for non-techie people like me.

4. Choose Keywords

Let's talk about how you know what keywords to bid on. There are three main strategies with choosing keywords:

1. Shotgun method
2. Copy and paste method
3. Mega Shotgun Method

Let's discuss the positives and negatives of each strategy.

1. Shotgun Method

In the shotgun method, you use tools like wordtracker. com, Google keyword, or the Adcenter/Google keyword suggestion tool to gather as many keywords as you think could apply to your market.

You then copy these words into your campaign or, if you are inside Adcenter/Google, you just click to "add key-words." You then do your best to target ads to these words, set your CPC bids, and go.

That's about it. You bid on a lot and hope something sticks. You try to attract as much traffic with as many key-words as possible, then adjust from there to only focus on what works.

This system does work. With this system, you need two main investments:

- Cash to blow through
- Endless hours to find winners/losers

Again, this system does work. There are many people teaching this method, and it's how I started out learning PPC. But I found this method to be very frustrating and cash-guzzling. I don't recommend this method for most people.

2. Copy and Paste Method

Do you like to copy and paste? I sure do.

I like to find shortcuts that save me time and make me more money. The copy and paste method is the one we use the most in our marketing efforts.

Here's how this method works. You simply use a tool

like Compete.com or KeywordSpy.com to find keywords your competitors are already bidding on.

Let's think about this for a second. If you track competing sites that have been advertising for six months or more on search engines, do you think they may have paused keywords that lose money by now? Probably. And, if they haven't yet, you will be able to put them on pause and know exactly what is making money so that you can blow your competitor out of the water. When you know which words to bid higher on and how to build winning campaigns around winning keywords, you become unstoppable.

Compete.com has a paid "pro" version, which I use all the time. Check out JeffUsner.com/bookbonus to see if there are any coupon codes, such as a code to get half off your first month's bill. This tool is worth a lot more than that.

Here's something I figured out about Compete.com, which has helped me make millions. At Compete.com, you can look at other competing websites and find out which keywords they are bidding on. This is similar to keyword-spy.com or any other keyword research tool. However, Compete.com takes it to another level. You can find all the keywords and then do a "sort" to rank them by "average time index."

The average time index will show you the keywords that caused users to stay on that competing website the longest. Do you think the more serious people on the website are on the website for a few seconds and gone, or are they the ones who stay the longest?

In most cases, if I could know which keywords caused people to stay on a website longer, those would probably point me to the money-making keywords. So this is exactly what you can do with this amazing tool.

Again, in an Excel spreadsheet or on the Compete.com

site, you click to sort by the column called "highest average time index" (how long people stayed on a website). Then copy and paste these keywords into your campaigns.

There is one other free tool I use before the paste part. I copy and paste the keywords into an "adwords wrapper." You can Google this term and find several websites offering this service for free. Basically, this tool does what we described previously for exact, phrase, and broad search matches. You copy and paste the words you want to bid on, and then the free adwords wrapper will give you each keyword in the proper format so that you can bid on all three types of phrases. Or, you can just use the exact and phrase matches. You then copy and paste these keywords into your keyword area of Google or Adcenter.

That's the copy and paste method.

3. Mega Shotgun Method

This is an advanced strategy where you bid on keywords based more on demographics than you do with the keywords matching your vertical or market. For example, if you sell cars, you could bid on every make, model, year, and color of every vehicle ever made. You would not be targeting a specific car buyer. You are simply looking to get people who are buying any kind of car to your website. This strategy is used to super-scale a campaign that appeals to a large audience. It does not work well for smaller niche products/ companies or services. This technique is for large audiences—such as weight loss, business opportunity, dating, skin care, and other highly competitive niches.

The method is based on the same type of strategies you would use to buy banner ads on different websites. You target keywords based on who would type them in. For example, with weight loss, this can be a very female-dominated market. One way would be to bid on other words that women looking to lose weight might be interested in, such as "celebrity gossip," "celebrity names," or other female-oriented keywords.

When you bid on words like this, you are using the mega shotgun technique. I'll go into this in much more depth later on in this book. Focus on method 1 or 2. I wanted you to be aware of this method as you scale, because it can bring you a ton of clicks and traffic. It's a different way of looking at search engines. Again, think laterally. Always think laterally. Can you buy media based on demographics across search engines? The answer is yes, you can.

Succeeding with Pay Per Click

Monitor like crazy

With PPC ads, you want to monitor them stringently; otherwise, you will lose a lot of money. It is important to set a daily budget on each campaign, say something like $5, and monitor it to see how it goes.

Scale up slowly

When you begin your campaigns in PPC or any form of advertising, it's usually best to start slowly, scaling up your budgets gradually so that you can refine your offer and traffic to be most profitable.

This applies to campaign budgets, but for bidding on cost per click (CPC), I usually start off with a high CPC bid so that I can get clicks to see if the traffic will work. CPC is basically the same as PPC. PPC or pay per click is a term to describe the type of marketing you are doing. Example, pay per click search marketing. The CPC is simply what you are actually paying to get these clicks. This is also what Google, Adcenter, and others will call it when you are bidding on a keyword. For a new keyword, I want to see if this is worth tweaking and scaling for profitability. The best way to do this is to get the traffic, and see if it converts. Once I know it converts, I can scale from there and focus on lowering my CPC bid. We will cover ramping an offer in a later chapter.

Once you set a bid and start to see traffic, you will want to gradually lower your bids by bidding 3 cents over the actual cost per click that you are paying. This is a process we have discovered where you will continue to hold a good position on your keyword/ad placement, and at the same time, lower your CPC (your spend). Again, the goal is to adjust our bids to keep our ranks high, but ultimately pay less for the clicks we are getting.

For example, take the term "wireless cell phone service." I may start bidding about $1 a click on this keyword (depending on how I see the competition doing and what the search engine research suggests). I would also probably set my budget low (depending on how large my overall budget is), but for just starting a new vertical, maybe I'd be willing to spend $25, $100, or $500 depending on the offer. It depends on how much the overall conversion of a click to a buyer is worth to me.

Then, as I begin to see clicks, maybe my actual cost per click might be 70 cents. Here's a point you need to understand. Your bid on your CPC is not necessarily what you are going to pay per click. The bid on the CPC simply tells Google or Adcenter, "hey, this is the most I am willing to pay for this click." Their system will then look at your bid versus other competitors to see what your actual cost will be. You never really know this until you run some live traffic through your site. Then, the search engine will show you what your actual cost per click is. After you see your actual CPC is 70 cents, you could change your $1 bid to 73 cents (just 3 cents over my actual cost per click). Again, I am not saying you should start your bidding at $1 CPC. This is simply an example of what you could do and how the process works.

Again, the goal with bidding just over the actual CPC is lower your click cost and maintain your traffic and position. We are trying to save you up to 50% or more on your traffic.

Keyword Setup

Let's get back to the ad setup. Naturally before you do this, you should have done your keyword research as described previously and in step 1 of Reverse Online Profits™ system.

Once you are logged in to Adcenter or Google, and you create a campaign and create an ad, you will be asked to add your keywords.

Other Search Engines

Setting up your PPC ads in other search engines is very simple, so it should be no trouble at all. The Adcenter has many videos to help you in boosting your Internet marketing efforts. There's a lot of decent stuff that can make you more money.

Bidding Strategies

Bid on:

- Domains

- TV commercials, radio, print media, TV shows domains

- Misspellings

- Geo targeting—include in the headline/ad. In this more advanced strategy, you are bidding on specific towns/areas with a keyword. For example, when I created traffic for people looking for "legal aid," I could add the keywords Austin, San Antonio, Dallas, Waco, etc., to the phrase to make it feel local. So the search result would read, Austin Legal Aid, San Antonio Legal aid, and so forth.

- Keyword insertion: This is a feature in Google.com or Adcenter.microsoft.com where the search engine will insert your keyword into a part of the ad, either your headline, body copy, url, or any and all of the above. This means every ad will show your keyword if you use this (as long as the keyword is not too long for the search engine to display). Each search engine gives you a limit on the number of characters you can type in the ad and headline. For example, if you did keyword insertion in your headline, and someone types in the words "Key Largo Lawyer", your ad headline would read "Key Largo Lawyer".

Advanced Strategies

- Set up multiple accounts for pure domination (separate companies)

- Set up multiple listings on money-making keywords

- Expand keywords in a working theme—for example, the keywords "apple," "core," "sweet," "crunchy" might all be part of the same theme.

- I would like to stress the importance of pre-selling everything at all times. I know I've said it before, but I want to repeat it, because to pre-sell traffic at all times is critical. The best thing to do is to get people ready to take action on whatever it is that you want them to take action on before they even get there. I repeat: get people ready for the next action before they arrive at the next step. Pre-selling is critical.

- It can be as simple as setting up your landing page, getting people to opt in, and doing your pre-sell. Get them to a product review website, and fill them in on personal stories regarding the use and effect of a product or service. It is really easy and most Internet marketers do not do it, because they are just lazy and lose their focus!

- Tips, Tips, and More Tips!

- Always test two to three ads minimum for highest CTR

- Don't get distracted — if PPC is working for you to generate revenue — think of other ways to scale this up

- Add similar keywords to a new campaign targeting the same goal as the current winning offer

- On bidding: While testing, start higher on bids, then monitor what your actual CPC is, and then adjust bid 3 cents above CPC

- Do this every few hours, depending on traffic

- Within 24-48 hours, your CPC can be down by as much as 50 percent

- Remember that a high CTR (click through rate) means lower CPC (cost per click)

- Test your ad position. Position No. 2 can make more money than No. 1 or No. 3 and vice versa. Whenever you see the search results for your keyword, you will see there are many ads displayed. We all know what it means to be No. 1 on the search engine. It is the top listing, but what about the ads below No. 1?

These also have tremendous value. You may be more profitable in ad position No. 2, but you must test this aspect of your marketing.

Compete With Yourself

Here is one strategy most people never use. They just don't get it. One of the fastest ways to make more money in any business is to simply compete with yourself. For example, if you have a PPC ad placed on one keyword, you might want to put up other PPC ads on the same thing, maybe three or four of them and compete with yourself.

This does a few good things for you. First, you monopolize the keyword, thereby keeping your competitors out. Second, you see which ad converts best for you. Just remember when you do this, you want to use different ads on different domains. Duplicate what works and just make money off it! It's really not hard to do, once you get the hang of it.

This sums up PPC ads and how to best implement this strategy into your business. Search has always been a great source of web traffic and will continue to be in the future. Now, let's learn about getting traffic from one of the top sites in the world, Facebook.com.

CHAPTER 6
How To Use Facebook

Mind-Boggling Growth

Did you ever think a website could grow to have close to 1 billion users in just a few short years? That's what Facebook did. To put that into perspective, Facebook.com will soon become the largest "nation" on the planet, meaning there will be more people on Facebook.com than those living in any one country.

Here are some stats on Facebook (reference http://infographiclabs.com/infographic/facebook-2012/):

- It has 845 million active users (as of February 2012).

- It accounts for 1 of every 5 page views on the Internet.

- Its users share more than 100 billion connections.

- More than 50 percent of North Americans use Facebook.

- 250 million photos are uploaded daily to the social network.

- There are more than 2.7 billion "likes" on Facebook every day.

- There are more than 425 million mobile users on Facebook.

That's mind-boggling. In this chapter, we are going to dive into how you can use Facebook to grow your relationships, expand your business, and make more money.

Facebook is one of the most powerful advertising mediums to ever exist. Let's focus on how you can productively use Facebook ads to build your credibility, build your brand, get leads, get sales, and increase profits.

In the last chapter, we explored how to use search engines to send massive amounts of traffic to your website. In this chapter, we are going to focus on using Facebook as the method of sending high volumes of traffic.

You are still in step 3 of the Reverse Online Profits™ system. We are focused on replicating/creating traffic to your website, and in this chapter we will look at Facebook traffic.

Ads Have Maximum Reach

First, to find ads on Facebook, simply login into your Facebook account and look on the right of almost any page you go to within Facebook. You will see ads with a headline (words) and an image below the headline. These ads are paid ads. Meaning, there are people paying for these ads to show up in front of you when you are in Facebook.

You might be wondering: Are Facebook ads effective? Can I really grow my business with Facebook? The simple answer is "yes." The complicated answer is "of course." Now let's discuss two ways to do this.

In the history of the Internet, there has never existed an advertising medium like Facebook. You can reach more people on Facebook than any other advertising medium on the planet; with search engines like Google, you are limited by keywords and the people searching for those keywords, but with Facebook, you can target anyone.

Whenever you start a new ad campaign on any medium, consider what your goal is. Who are you targeting? Why does the audience want what you have? Do you want to make a sale? Do you want to just brand yourself? Do you want to get "likes"? Do you want leads? What do you want?

You need to be clear about your goal as you start to set up your Facebook ad campaign.

Targeting Works

The money is in the targeting, and here's what that means. Whenever anyone logs into Facebook, he or she will see ads on the right side of the page that are 100 percent tailored to who they are.

In other words, if I go to Facebook.com, and my wife has been on my computer using her Facebook account, the first thing I notice—that makes me know I'm not logged in as myself—is that the ads are all different than the ones I am used to seeing. Why?

The first ad I see is for "women's sandals." The second ad is about becoming a "pre-school teacher," the third one is for "Paxil birth defects," and the fourth ad has a headline of "women entrepreneurs."

OK, let's take a step back.

If I were a male (which I am), would I usually click on any of these ads? No! These ads are targeting women, more specifically those in my wife's age range (can't disclose that!) and her potential "likes" or interests.

If I were logged into my own Facebook account, the ads would be targeting males in their 30s, and maybe someone interested in marketing. I would see ads for topics around my likes.

What ads do you see? Do the ads appeal to you? Start to pay attention to who is advertising to you. Maybe this is where you can get an idea for a business. That wouldn't be a big surprise, because Facebook is showing you ads about things you might be interested in. You might see an ad and say to yourself, "I could do that." If so, jot the idea down.

Are you starting to understand the power of Facebook? You can target people based on:

- Male/Female

- Single/Engaged/Married/In a relationship

- State/Country/Zip code/City

- Age

- Interests

- College Grad/In college/In high school

- Where they work

How to Target

Let's look at an example of how this can be so powerful. Let's say I am a local mortgage loan officer. I live in a small town. The market is slow, and I need a way to get more business.

I could run an ad in my zip code or around my city that targets people who graduated from the University of Texas (Longhorns). I could use a picture of a "Bevo," the mascot for the Longhorns, and write a headline like "Refinance Special: Get Cash."

In the subheadline, I could write, "Longhorns fan? Want to get some money out of your home?" Or something to this effect. The point is I can be very specific in two areas:

1. The image I use

2. The words I use

Let's say I use a picture of the Bevo mascot (most Texas grads would know this) and said "hey, Longhorn fans!" These are two elements in an ad that would get my attention if I were a Texas graduate.

I could also target my ad to "college graduates" since I don't want kids who are still in school. I want people out of school with some extra money. I could also target a certain age range so that I would get people in their late 20s or maybe first-time homebuyers or those who have only owned a home for a few years.

Take another example.

Let's say I live in the Austin, Texas, area, which has a lot of people employed by Dell. I could choose specific zip codes to run ads in. If I am a pizza shop owner, I could run an ad with a Dell image (depending on copyright laws) or something "Dell" (that a Dell employee would recognize) and say, "Dell employees, Get 2 Pizzas for the price of 1" or something like that.

Again, my ad is running in my backyard and is targeting certain people. I could probably get these clicks very cheaply. The result could mean thousands of dollars in sales for a small investment. I could go a level deeper and even target certain fraternities and sororities at the University of Texas. There is no limit to how you target and how to approach each of these potential markets.

That's why Facebook ads are so powerful. It's like buying banner space on a website where you know the exact demographic and your ad only displays to those who meet your needs 100 percent.

Where else can you target an ad to someone who lives in your zip code, who is 34, who likes Golden retrievers, who is engaged, who has a college degree, who was in a certain sorority, who likes Starbucks Caramel Macchiato, who doesn't like the current president, who loves Michael Jackson, who reads the Bible, who loves the movie The Notebook, who loves snowboarding, who works at Dell, and whose birthday is today? This is possible, because Facebook has all this info and will use it to target your ad specifically.

We could go even deeper in our targeting, but if I wanted to target this specific of a demographic (female, 34, local, loves coffee, loves dogs, etc.) I could even run an ad with a picture/image of something that matches what she loves. This is powerful, because your response rates can go through the roof.

The "interest" targeting part is the real killer here. It is not just targeting — IT IS TARGETING ON STEROIDS!

You could also target fan pages where your customers might hang out. Gurus, competitors' fan pages, weight watchers, health pages, quilting fan pages, motorcycle fan pages, anything!

Consider all the things people tell through Facebook about themselves: age, gender, education, marital status, pets, friends, political interest, background, likes or interests, and so much more — it's crazy! People are willing to hand over all the information you could possibly ever want to know about them. (Think about that next time you are on Facebook.) And Facebook can use that information to make as much money as possible for itself. The privacy policy on Facebook is pretty scary. You give the company the rights to do almost anything with your information, photos, videos, etc.

So how do you use this information to make money in your business?

First, I suggest you do what I've shared throughout this book. Find someone or a company doing what you want to do, and see where they are advertising on Facebook. How do you do this?

1. After you find a website (step 1) that is a competitor or potential market, you take that website and plug it into Compete.com or Quantcast.com and look at the site's demographics.

2. Then use/login to someone's Facebook account that matches that demographic. Ask one of your friends to see if you can login to see the ads. (Pay them $5.00 if you have to…)

3. Go to Facebook.com/ads/adboard to see what is

being advertised to this demographic. (Also, look at JeffUsner.com/bookbonus to find some great paid services, which monitor all the advertising on Facebook based on any demographic.)

The key with the above three steps and launching ads on Facebook is to put yourself in the shoes of your target market. If are you targeting people who love dogs, consider what types of dogs they might like and what types of interests they may have. Same thing goes with any vertical.

If you have a product to market to people with a home business, what interests do they have, who do they follow already, do they like their own company, do they like a certain trainer, do they like a certain system, and are they part of a certain group?

So that is exactly what you do on your Facebook account. You basically become somebody else.

Tweak your profile to add the demographic that you want for your product/service, throw in some likes and interests, and instantly you will see different ads on the right side of your page. Or go to Facebook ad boards to see more ads! You do not even have to do this yourself. Again, you can outsource this for very little money and, in exchange, get valuable research for money-making campaigns on Facebook! I'll teach more about this in the chapter on outsourcing.

There's one thing you should remember with Facebook ads. The networking site gets its users to approve or reject ads, so you might want to save a copy of your ad on a notepad in case it gets rejected. If it gets rejected, just submit it again; after a few hours it will get accepted. It has to do with the human approval process that the site uses, so naturally what is acceptable to one may not be to another, so just go ahead and try again. One thing that works is to set up an ad that is similar to another previously accepted ad, and within minutes it goes live.

Important: Because people are not on Facebook to buy, it's crucial to that your ad is not too sales-y. You want to look different but not by doing a sales pitch. In your marketing efforts, your goal should be to give valuable information or content. Keep this focus on Facebook, and you will do better than most companies.

Create Explosive Ads

The most important aspect of any ad on Facebook is the image you use. I believe 80 percent of the ad's effectiveness is the image. Always attempt to use an image that will get the attention of the person you are marketing to, such as an image of a college mascot if you are targeting that college, as in my previous example. You could use a picture of someone in a uniform of the company. For example, show a man dressed in a brown UPS-type outfit if your ad is targeting UPS employees. This will get their attention.

Some quick pointers/nuggets:

- If you can use a "play" button on an image in the ad, do it.

- If you can add a border to an ad, do it. Bright red tends to work the best.

- Funny and out-of-the-ordinary pictures get people's attention.

- Running ads that lead to other Facebook pages versus on another website will get cheaper clicks. (meaning when you click on the ad, do you stay within Facebook or go to an outside website.)

- Start running an ad in the evening (after most people are through their ad budgets; you'll get cheaper clicks).

- Set an ad budget.

- Rotate headlines.

- Rotate images.

- Monitor CTR of ads.

- Put words on the image.

Search on Google images for non-copyrighted images to use in your ads. TEST, TEST, TEST.

Here are some ways to find demographics of any competitor on Facebook:

- Just go to "create an ad."

- Pick competitor's name/company as a "like."

- See the number of people who like them.

- Change the age range, sex, etc., and see how it changes the number.

- This will show you the main number of people in their exact demographics.

You can then use this information by running ads to these demographics. This will lead to your ads having a higher CTR, which means you will get a lower CPC.

Lower your ad cost by as much as 50% or more. You could change an ad to CPM (cost per thousand impressions).

This is a different strategy in which you don't bid on clicks, but you bid on the number of times your ad is shown, regardless of whether someone clicks on it.

It is an advanced strategy to change an ad from a CPC bid to a CPM bid. A CPM bid means you are bidding an amount to show your ad 1,000 times to people on Facebook. Only do this when you have an ad with a very high CTR.

For example, let's say you have an ad that shows a CTR of 0.04 percent. This would mean that every time your ad displays 1,000 times, you are averaging 40 clicks. If you are set up on a CPC basis and you are paying 50 cents a click, this would cost you $20 for the 40 clicks. So you are paying $20 for your ad to show 1,000 times. Here's the crazy part. You might be able to create the same ad, (use the "create similar ad" option when setting up the ad in Facebook) and just set the ad to a CPM bid basis versus CPC. You might be able to bid $1 CPM and get the same amount of traffic. And if your CTR stayed the same at 0.04 percent, you would get 40 clicks for the $1 bid you made on the 1,000 impressions. You could potentially cut your ad cost by up to 95 percent!

Interruption Marketing

You must remember why people are on Facebook. The bottom line is they are there to be social. They are not really there to find a solution to their problems or to buy things. The key is to get inside their minds and find out who are they, what they like, what they believe in, and then serve it to them.

The beauty of Facebook is that it is very easy to get leads and fans if you use short-form lead capture pages (websites that only ask for a little information for people to submit) that have to do with education, games, dating, insurance, debt, zip or email submits, and other similar things. If you are building your business, you could drive traffic from your Facebook ads to:

- Fan pages
- Lead capture forms
- Videos
- Webinar registrations (get name and email) and
- More.

The key is to decide upfront what your goal is. Then design a marketing funnel to cater to that goal. And always remember one of the most important aspects of any marketing:

Test!

Like everything else, the rule is to test, test, and test. This rule applies to any medium where you place advertisements. Split test your ads; for the same ad, use different headlines and images to which draws the most response, and rotate your ads often.

Banner Blindness

Because Facebook users spend an average 20 minutes per session on the site, one of the biggest challenges you run into is something called "banner blindness." This is what happens after someone sees your ad too many times. They don't really "see" it after a certain number of times and your ad becomes "blind" to them. They will stop clicking on the same ad. So you must rotate ads, keep them fresh, and use different images often.

To avoid banner blindness, you can:

- Try new image

- Try new headline

- Try geo split test (Different locations)

- Try new border on image

- Just pause it, sometimes for a few days or a week, and then unpause

- You can build up a rotation of ads to pause/unpause

- Do not set it and forget it like PPC

More Nuggets

- Brainstorming is key. There are tons of things available on Facebook and this translates into massive opportunities. Target various interests and you can build a massive opt-in list using Facebook by giving away free content. You can outsource this content or maybe find a website that provides the same free information and serve it to your target audience! Easy!

- Just as in PPC, it is important to set your daily budget on your Facebook ads and monitor it. For your initial bid, set it 3 cents over what Facebook suggests to get to the top and see what happens, and maybe after half an hour, go back to lower your bid if things are converting.

- Be sure to follow Facebooks Adverising guidelines because Facebook can ban your advertising account with no notice to you. Don't be too sales-y, check your spelling, avoid bad language and bad images. Basically just watch everything that you say and do! Be honest. Deliver good value and content.

- Focus on narrow niches and interests so you can tailor your offers to your target audience. If you talk the talk of your prospective clients, it increases your CTR and decreases your CPC!

Use Facebook for Branding

You can use Facebook to brand yourself. You can take a different approach from wanting to create leads and sales, and instead focus on branding who you are.

You basically create a "billboard" on Facebook where you are not as focused on the clicks, but on getting and keeping your face or brand in front of Facebook users.

Here's how this works. Let's say you are a local beautician. You could create an ad on Facebook with your face/brand. The ad's goal could be to make a sale, like we have already discussed. The ad might say, "Attention [insert your town] Ladies, 50% off special on all haircuts, color and waxing." Or something like this to generate sales in your area. This works.

But what if you just wanted to brand yourself so that every time you went to the supermarket, every time you were out in public in your area, people would recognize you? They would know your face. They would associate your face with a great hairdresser.

Here's how you could do that. You could target women in your zip code or area again. (You could apply this within industries/gurus/tradeshows/ etc. as well.) This time your ad might just read "Your Company Name" with a picture of your face. And the words on the ad could say, "The Best Hairdresser in [Your Town], Limited Appointments Available" or something like this. You may not get a ton of clicks, but you could start pounding into people's minds who you are and that you are the best at whatever it is you do. You could target women's groups in your area, or a women's gathering the week before they meet so that when you show up, people know who you are and what you do.

Again, this is branding with a "billboard" on Facebook. You may not get a ton of clicks, as that is not the goal. But you could get 200,000 impressions in your local area if your ad was displayed to the 10,000 women in your city just 20 times, and it might only cost you a few hundred dollars or more. Impressions simply means the number of times your ad is seen. So if your ad had 200,000 impressions, this means people saw your ad 200,000 times.

I don't know of any billboards that:

1. Cost a few hundred dollars;

2. Would get you that many targeted/relevant impressions (people seeing you).

Who do you think these women are going to think of next time they need a haircut? Or the next time they have to wait too long for their current hairdresser? Or the next time their kids get a bad haircut? They will probably be thinking of you. This gets your phone ringing and business in the door. And on Facebook, you have the power of word-of-mouth advertising. You become a rock star in your local community.

The opportunities with Facebook ads are limitless. Monitor what others are doing. Look for ideas from different markets to apply to your market. As always, find someone doing something similar on Facebook to what you want to do and learn from them. This is an important piece in step 3 of the Reverse Online Profits™ system. Facebook is one of the best online advertising resources that you have access to for replicating and creating major traffic to your website.

Now let's continue to step 4 of the ROP system, which will focus on converting all these visitors to your website into dollars for your business. With this next step, I have been able to make close to $120,000 an hour. Let's get to it.

CHAPTER 7

Build Your Following

A few years ago, my wife and I were on a flight from Pittsburgh to Dallas. It was a Sunday night, and we had just spent the entire weekend at an amazing event. We were drained. During most of the flight, I was in relaxation mode, just taking it easy.

As we approached Dallas, the pilot made an announcement on the PA system.

He said, "Good evening, everyone. This is your captain. I wanted to give you a brief update on our flight status. Right now, we are still cruising at 35,000 feet. It's a smooth ride so far, but we are about to encounter a few bumps. There's a huge mass of thunderstorms around Dallas and we are going to circle Dallas a few times to see if this clears up so we can make a landing. If not, we are getting low on fuel and we may have to veer off to Houston to refuel. I'm sorry for the inconvenience. Hopefully, we'll have you on the ground shortly. Thank you."

Great, I thought. Long weekend and exhausted. What do we do?

This flight offered Wi-Fi service. I hadn't used it before, as I didn't like the idea of spending $10 to use the Internet for just an hour or so. You can only use it above 10,000 feet, and on many flights it seems like by the time you get a snack or drink, you are already landing.

Anyway, I decided after the announcement that I'd pay to get on the Internet. But, I would only do it under one condition. I had to make money while we were circling Dallas.

The fastest way I knew to make money was to send an email.

How long does it take to send an email? Two to five minutes maximum, right?

So I logged into one of our email accounts. I found an affiliate offer I could share with one of our lists. This took about two minutes. I typed out a few words and hit "send." That was it.

I didn't think about it after that, other than reasoning that I would at least make the $10 back I spent to get on the Internet.

Eventually, our plane landed in Dallas. We missed our connection and got stuck there, arriving at a hotel around 2 a.m. This was just in time to grab a few hours of sleep before our flight early the next morning.

By the time we caught the next flight and got home, it was Monday afternoon. I hadn't thought much about the email I had sent. I was simply excited to be home with my kids. Spending time with them was my primary focus.

As the day progressed and turned to night, we finally got the kids to bed. That's when I decided to open my laptop to see how that little email was doing. After all, it had taken me about five minutes to send it while cruising at about 35,000 feet in Texas. Anyway, technology is amazing to me. In what other business could you be delayed while on an airplane, but be able to log on the Internet and send an email? It's amazing.

What was even more amazing was when I checked out

the stats of how that email did. What I saw on the screen, it made me do a "double take." I thought there must be some mistake. It showed that my total earnings—only 24 hours after sending the email—were about $6,000.

Six thousand dollars for about five minutes of work! That translates to $120,000 an hour. That still blows me away today. An email list is an asset for life.

In business and in life, I've learned that building assets is much better than building liabilities. Would you rather invest your time and energy into something that will pay you once, or would you rather invest your time into something that could pay you for years and years to come?

Step 4 in our Reverse Online Profits™ system is focused on building assets. It's like when I was at 35,000 feet and used a current asset—an email database—to make the most money possible at that moment. Let's recap where you are in the ROP system.

In this chapter we are going to focus on step 4 of the ROP system. You will learn how to build a list in any niche/market/product/service you want.

There are basically two types of lists you can build:

1. Relationship-based list

2. Non-relationship-based list

In the relationship-based list, you are focused on building a brand, a retail business, a service, or product. You want to form a relationship with your clients so they continue to come back to you for your products/services/brand.

The non-relationship-based model focuses on building a larger database and simply monetizing the list without ever building a brand or relationship.

Both types of lists are very valuable and can make you and your company a lot of money. Both lists usually deal with giving something for free to a market or niche, or filling a need users have, in exchange for them "opting in" (filling out a form with their name, email, and in some cases more information).

There are several ways to do this. However, in this chapter we will focus on the top strategies to grow your business and your list. When you start to think of all the different markets that exist online, you simply have to give them something they want so you can build a list in any vertical.

For example, in the relationship list method, here's how Nike.com might use this strategy with you, their client.

Let's say you go to Nike.com to buy some shoes. While you are on the website, Nike might offer you special updates or maybe a coupon code and tell you the company will email it to you. Along with the special offer or coupon, you're also asked if you'd like to receive any other updates on products you may like. Most times, people say yes.

When we do this, we give Nike our email and name, and now Nike has an opportunity for years to come to follow up with us with special promotions, coupons, offers, or more via email.

This may not sound like much to you, but imagine now for a moment their website is your website. And, let's say that each time someone visits your website they give you their contact information, such as their name and email.

OK, great, now what?

Now, you can follow up with every person on a daily, weekly, or monthly basis and offer them more of your products or services or just offer them free information.

In the relationship list method, you are able to quickly accomplish a major marketing goal. You are able to establish yourself as an authority to the consumer. This can set you up to earn income for life.

Take another example. Let's say you are a doctor or chiropractor who helps people with back pain. If you were to do the research as taught in previous chapters, you would find there are a lot of people constantly searching for help with back pain. In fact, you could find some people/companies making a lot of money helping people solve back pain.

If you wanted to enter this market and become a branded authority, you might set up a website where your focus is helping people with quick solutions to relieve back pain. You could create some videos and/or a report showing/telling people what to do for fast back-pain relief.

Do you think if you could help people get over some back pain, they would be open to you sharing information on anything else? Of course. This works in any market. Help people solve a problem and they will love you! We'll take this example a step further in a moment when we talk about becoming the authority in a market.

Developing a list is one of the most valuable assets you can have on the Internet. This is why step 4 of ROP can be so critical to your long-term business growth. Regardless of what business you are in, your list of clients or potential clients is the most valuable resource you have.

The amazing thing is you can set up almost the entire process on autopilot. Here's how it works.

- People visit your website.

- They give you their information (email and name).

- You email them what you told them you would. (This can be 100 percent automated.)

- They receive a series of valuable information and offers for years to come.

- Every email makes you money, because someone on the list will buy!

You might be thinking, "This just can't be." But, I say it's true. I know countless business owners who have used this strategy to create major financial leverage in their lives.

One of the hidden benefits of the Reverse Online Profits™ system is the power of leverage. You can leverage yourself through advertising on the Internet, which runs whether you work or not. You can have people coming to your website whether you get out of bed in the morning or not. You could have people coming to your websites while you sleep, while you are with your kids, or sitting on some remote beach in Bora Bora.

Leverage is key to building wealth. You can leverage yourself through advertising and through building a list of people who are interested in what you have to offer. Again, this works for any business online or offline.

However, the great thing about the Internet is that most

of the list relationship and monetization can happen for you on autopilot once you set it up.

I have a friend named Jeremy. When he first started his online business he had amazing success. One of the exciting things he did was build a list of people. After some time, his primary business stopped doing well. I remember talking with him about what he could do to improve on what he had done in the past.

As we discussed his business, it came out that although he built a list, he hadn't been emailing the people on it. The first thing I told him to do was to go send them an email.

He did that, and I believe his first email made several hundred dollars. He continued to email that list and made money every time.

This is the power of building a list. It's literally like printing money every time you hit "send."

There are several companies that make this process very easy. I won't go into great detail here on how to use them, but you can find them at jeffusner.com/bookbonus. These are companies that make it very easy to collect your market's information (name & email) and to follow up with the users effortlessly and on autopilot.

Let's get into more of the dynamics of list building and how you can profit wildly from this simple step in the Reverse Online Profits™ system.

Money Is in the Relationship

With the relationship-based method, here's the reality: the money is in the relationship, not in the list. It does not matter how many lists you have or how many emails are a part of one single list you have. You'll be surprised that there are thousands of Internet marketers out there who have built lists over time, but they are not making money with these lists.

I wish I was kidding but really I am not . . . these people don't understand this basic principle.

Because the truth is that the money is not in the list but in how you use your list and the relationship you build with the people on it. One thing for you to figure out in your business is that people don't buy products, people buy you! If they like working with you, they will buy from you for life!

You may have a list with a million people, but if you don't build a relationship with that list, or worse, if you do not even know how to use it, you will not make any money. The best way to start a business relationship is to give first. When you can give a solution to a problem for free, your list (people) will be very open to whatever else you have to share, because you have given them something and helped them. You have built some trust with them.

The best way to build long-term wealth with a list, using the relationship-list method, is to establish your product/service/company as the go-to authority in the marketplace you are in. This may not seem easy, but we are going to lay out a quick, simple method to do this within the next thirty to sixty days in any market.

Become the Authority in Your Market

- Find out what your market needs badly. What is the biggest problem the audience faces every day?

- Give them the answer/solution to this problem.

- Use video to establish your brand

- Use Facebook to got viral and build social proof by gathering success stories of people using your solution and the results they got.

- Share those success stories.

It's not too hard to become an expert in any field today. The reason is that 99.9 percent of your competition will never employ the simple five steps above. These steps may not seem simple to you yet, but after we walk through how you do this, you can get this plan into action today. It's not too hard to stand out from the crowd on the Internet.

With a video camera and a little market research, you can have any market wanting more of what you have. The great part about this process is you can hire or outsource the creation of the solution to the problems you find. Even if you know nothing about the solution, you could be marketing the piece behind the "solution."

What you will find is there are many experts in many markets. However, very few experts actually have a clue about how to market their business/knowledge and expertise. Believe it or not, you can hire people with doctorates to write papers for you for a few hundred dollars (not that you need a PhD to become an authority).

You might think there is a huge need for "boat repair." You may know nothing about boat repair, but you know someone who can repair boats or you can simply find someone who can repair them. You could offer to pay them $100 for four to six hours of their time to show you the most common repairs on boats. You could get permission to videotape them and own the video rights. Now go out and offer people with boats (a Facebook interest of many) this information on how to fix their boats. Then you could build a huge list of boat owners.

A list of boat owners could be very valuable. Next, you

could create some follow-up content to share with them (maybe from your boat repair source) or you could have a list of thousands of people and simply go out to a boat company and say, "I have a few thousand people who would love to learn about your boats. Would you be interested in me sending them to you to find out about your boats?" If they say yes, you could respond with, "Great, what we could do is you could just pay me per person I send to you or you could simply pay me a 15 percent commission on each sale." You could work out something like this.

Boat owners usually have expendable cash flow. You could promote another person's boat accessory website and get paid to drive your clients to their site.

You could create a website for boat owners to talk to each other. You could put valuable content on the website that boat owners would love and start to create a brand that people go to in order to be part of a "boating community." You could then sell advertising on your site or simply put Google Adsense on your site. I don't know for sure, but I would imagine Google might pay out even $1 to $3 a click off ads targeted at boat owners. Now just generate a few thousand clicks a week to your website through an email, and you could be making close to a six-figure residual income from a market you are not an expert in.

Does this make sense? You don't need to be the expert. But, you can be if you want to be. It's up to you. Building a list and a following is simple. It's one of the most profitable activities you could do in business. You are building customer databases. This is why companies are sold for a lot of money. The reason Facebook.com is worth so much is because of the number of followers/users on the website. You can do the same thing on a smaller scale and still make thousands or millions of dollars in extra income.

Once you develop yourself or your brand as the authority, you are able to build a long-term, stable business in any market or niche.

Next, you create a fan page on Facebook and allow your fans to follow the page. They will share your fan page with others and you could start to communicate with your followers on Facebook. You could post on Facebook information about your "boat website" and drive all kinds of traffic to your site. This is the exact method we have followed in several markets where we sometimes earn more than $2,000 a day in Adsense. It's not hard to do; it just takes some initiative to go do it.

When you add success stories from people sharing on Facebook to your marketing efforts and videos, it puts your marketing on steroids!

Now, imagine doing this in one new vertical a month. Once you get the traffic streams set up, you can literally sit back while most of the business runs on autopilot. The even better news is you can outsource and pay someone about $1-$2 an hour to do most of the hard work.

The Internet is all about lifestyle to me. You can earn millions of dollars or thousands of dollars—it's up to you. And you can do both on a very part-time basis as your business grows.

Let's talk about non-relationship-based list building.

When you create non-relationship-based lists, you are simply building offers or websites where you want to collect some data to follow up with the audience at a later time with other email offers, which may have nothing to do with the main reason they originally contacted your company.

This doesn't require relationship building, and the monetization (earning power) of your list can be 100 percent outsourced to a few select companies that will then send you a check for 50 percent of the revenue. There are many companies who focus on monetizing data full time. This is their business. Any information you can give them, they will use to make the money for you and for them. It's a great deal for both of you so you can focus on creating data and they can focus on making money with that data.

This is a model our company has used very successfully. It can generate up to an additional $50,000 to $200,000 a month.

You can also send out your own emails to these lists of people and keep 100 percent of the profits. You just need to invest time learning the legalities of CAN-SPAM laws to make sure you are doing this right. CAN-SPAM laws were creating to stop spammers. I would suggest you Google "CAN SPAM laws" to get more legal counsel on this matter.

Again, you can do this, especially on a small scale, but as you send more and more email, it might be best to outsource this part and simply focus on creating front-end offers where you collect more and more data to make money with.

You need to pick your battles. You need to pick where your time is best spent and then focus there.

A few more tips on relationship list building:

- Take time to build a relationship upfront before you promote a lot of your products or other people's products.

- Invest time/resources by giving people on your list valuable content so they keep coming back and waiting for your emails.

- Write your emails in a way that you are "training" people to click links in your emails

- Start "training" your list to click on free videos and free content

- When you send an email later about another product where you could make a commission, your CTR on your emails will be through the roof and you'll make a lot more money long term.

Learn From My Mistakes

I know I sound like a list-building professional, but believe me, my first foray into list building is not exactly all pretty in pink. For years and years, I built my list on yellow post-it notes. I call myself the post-it-note king. My desk, walls and floors were covered with yellow post it notes with people's names, phone numbers, emails and more. The names were scattered, and unorganized.

I was horrible at follow up because I would lose all my contact's information. If the people on my list weren't interested in my primary product or service, I'd never contact them again. That was a big mistake because I was never able to market anything else to them for the rest of my life.

You must keep every name and email of every person you are able to market to. I did not keep thousands of people's information, and I am sure I lost a ton of money because of it. In the past, I would have people's information all over my desk and office, losing it, not tracking it, and not monetizing it. That's not the case anymore.

So a cardinal rule: get a central location to keep all of your leads, lists, and opt-ins. Don't be stupid! The importance of capturing names and emails cannot be stressed enough when it comes to providing you with an ongoing income. The potential is huge, so you have to focus and get your act together for this one. We recommend several services to help you do this at JeffUsner.com/bookbonus. You can use these services regardless of what type of business you start or currently operate.

Make Your Emails Pay You Automatically

Would you like money flowing into your bank account on auto pilot? I used to dream of this, and finally figured out how to make this a reality. And, the main way I use to do this is by simply setting up emails that pay me automatically. Here's how this works. On the Internet, there are many services for setting up autoresponders. Autoresponders are simply emails that you load in a system, which automatically sends these emails out for you to your prospects on the days you want the emails to go out. So if you set up 365 straight days of emails to go out to your list, your autoresponder will send these emails to every lead you ever generate without you ever having to click "send." This can mean everyday an email is going out to your list of people whether you are sleeping, vacationing, working, or whatever you are doing. These emails make you money on auto pilot in any business.

This is a powerful way to grow a huge backend income in any business. This has worked tremendously for me. Also, when you develop your email marketing to your list, it gives you an unfair advantage when paying for traffic on the Internet. You can pay more than anyone else because you can make money with every contact or lead you generate. More money means you can buy more advertising. When you figure out how much each person or lead is worth to you over the first year and lifetime in your database, you become unstoppable.

Our companies compete in some highly competitive

markets. We are able to blow away a lot of our competitors because we understand the long-term value of each lead we create. Again, there are many companies we recommend for setting up autoresponder messages. (Please check our website at jeffusner.com/bookbonus, because these can change over time.) The reason this can change is some companies do a great job at getting your emails into inboxes, and then all of a sudden, every email you send winds up in a spam box and you aren't making any money. So keep up to date on these by checking out our resources area.

The Best Way to Create a List

There are many ways to build a list, but the best way is by giving away free information. More specifically, free information, which solves a problem your market is facing. People love anything with the word "free" attached to it, but when it is 'free' combined with the solution to a problem they have, that is a winning formula.

You simply start at solving a problem. What's the biggest problem in your market? Figure that out, then give your market the answer.

The free content (answer) you offer can be delivered in many formats. Ebooks, video, audio, webinars, online meetings, books, and more. However, the easiest way to create content is to simply pick up your iphone or video camera, and have someone film you discussing a solution to a problem your market is facing.

For example, if you are targeting someone in a home business, you can give them a book saying "Free guide to make $1,000 more today!" Or, if you are in the weight loss niche, you can say "Free report reveals 7 healthy foods that are making you fat!" This can be applied to any product, service, or industry. You look at the what the market wants, then give it to them.

This free, valuable content that you provide can come from you or you could hire a content writer or expert. You don't even have to be the one giving them the answer. You can simply send them a link to a video on Youtube.com or a website with an article which solves the problem. Do you understand this? You don't have to be the one (or expert) to solve the problem. Let someone else solve the problem, and you build a list which becomes a huge asset for you for life!

Offer Value

In creating your autoresponder emails, the most important thing is to give value, then do some reviews, give more content, and then present what you want to offer. For instance, you can send out a few emails addressing the problem someone has, and then send out a quick email a few days later saying something like:

Hey (firstname),
Jeff here again.
I hope the last few emails I sent out helped you with (put the problem you solved).
I might be able to help you another way…
Since you are focused on making more money from home -
I thought you might find this website interesting. It shows a way for you to make extra $500 to $1,000 a month in your business without changing anything. . . .
Check it out here.
Have a great day!
Jeff

Sounds pretty simple, right?
But the key to nailing this is to offer value before you

discuss any opportunities to buy from you or anyone you recommend. When you offer people value for free, you earn their trust. Find out what they want first, who they are, and then give them what they want. Give away your best free stuff and people will love you and follow you for life!

Once you have a list, the possibilities are endless. But one thing you should do is determine the value of a subscriber. How much is a new lead (opt in) worth to you for the next year, two years, etc. Figure this out as soon as possible, because this information helps you know how much you can invest to get a lead.

When you know your metrics, you become dangerous! Know thy numbers!

Let me show you an example of how you can keep money rolling from your list:

For example, let's say you build a website about baby names. You could build a list of people by creating a valuable service of letting people search popular baby names. If you apply the principle of thinking laterally, you can send your list similar offers that expecting mothers would like. You could even get their due dates and then send out valuable information and resources after their due date. We've had a lot of babies in my house! So, I've seen this method work very well in the mail. It seems right after another baby is born, there is something in our mailbox to get us into some products. Baby food, baby diapers, formula, you name it, all in our mailbox. You could do the exact same thing online and make even more money.

Once you build a list, sending emails gets really fun. It's great to write an email in a few minutes, then set it up in your autoresponder and know that email could make you thousands every month or day! They take around five to ten minutes to compose, and they can give you hundreds or even thousands of dollars in return! Just click "send" and your income can skyrocket. Can you think of anything more fun to watch?

The Secret to Emails that Make Money

As with any marketing piece you ever do, and email is no different: before you send or even write an email, ask yourself what the goal of the email is. You have to set a particular goal that you want that email to accomplish. This is key, or else why even write the email if it leads nowhere? Picture what you want to accomplish first and then get there!

So if your goal is to inform a person, educate a person, and then get a click to a website, you'll write the email a certain way. You'll give people good content they would want to read, and then give them a way to find out more.

Sometimes, you just write an email with a great headline to create interest to drive traffic to your website, where you can deliver more information. Plus, when someone gets to your website, you now control the environment better and can direct them to where you want them to go or take the action you want them to take.

Subject Lines Are the "Secret Sauce."

You also have to work on your subject lines, because they are the key that opens the money door.

If you don't write a good subject line, your email will be in the trash before it's had a chance to work. So your subject lines must be killer. They must arouse curiosity like no other, because at the beginning, the primary goal is to get the email opened!

How do you know which subject lines work best? A stream of testing ought to do it! As I mentioned, there are some great companies we can recommend you send your email to. These email software services usually have robust statistical reporting, yet they are easy to use. Most can show you within one to two clicks what made you the most money or got you the response you wanted to get.

Let me share something with you I have tried that gave me very high open rates of my emails. Two words: "bad news..."

This subject line works very well, but you have to be careful how you use it. You don't want to scare people and then not really have an explanation for the 'bad news'. This subject is really something that people scramble to open, because, believe it or not, people want to know about bad news more than good news! Crazy, right?

Pre-Sell with Email

We have talked about pre-selling in your advertising with Facebook or Search, but it's also critical in your email marketing. The rule does not change in writing emails. It is important to pre-sell everything. It is better to pre-qualify than just get clicks. Ask yourself, what do you want to let them know before they arrive at the website you are directing them to?

Email Goals

There are two types of reasoning in email goals and pre-selling:

- **Soft qualifier:** emails are short; the goal is to catch the interest of the target customers and get them to click through a website, which spills all the beans.

- **Hard qualifier:** tends to be longer emails where details are clearly shared. Usually these get fewer clicks, but these are quality clicks and, in terms of conversions, quality clicks can be higher.

When you are sending people to another website from your email, remember that the name of the game is all about congruency. You want to make people feel and think that they are in the right place. For example, you can put the subject line as a headline on the website they will arrive at to achieve this goal. Conversion will be higher!

Fast Money-Maker

Invite your list to be social, and you make money.

You can use your emails to promote your Facebook fan page or send an autoresponder email day one and two inviting your list to get social. You can easily build your "likes" and fans through email.

Here's one final key to writing any email or marketing piece. And, this may be one of the most important parts of this book. (you found here at the end of Chapter 7.)

When you write, always write to one person. You need to decide who you are writing to. What is the demographic of your market? Are you writing to a woman, a male, old, young, married, single, in school, out of school, etc. You need to speak to that one person in all you do.

When you write like this, the person reading your email or marketing will feel like you are talking directly to them. So don't start out an email addressed to 'many people'. Would you read an email addressed to a group of people or one catered specifically to you?

Write to one person. For example, in this book, I am writing to a few target audiences. One of those audiences is someone who is new in business, male, 25-45 years old, someone with children, married and looking to improve their life. This may or may not be you. But, most of this book was written with me 'pretending' this person is sitting right across from me. I am speaking directly at this person.

There are also a few other demographics I am writing to, so don't feel left out! I am writing to you too, if you don't fit that demographic above.

One way I am able to focus on this is to simply put a post it note up in front of me with a description of the person I am writing to. Try it, it works!

Learning how to build a list and how to communicate to your list is one of the highest-paid professions in the world. And, you can do it from anywhere in the world, anytime of day, and put most of it on autopilot.

Next, we will continue in the Reverse Online Profits™ system and show you how to take a losing, cash-sucking campaign and turn it into your blue-ribbon, first-prize cash cow! That's what ramping and banking is all about.

CHAPTER 8
Know When To Hold 'em & Fold 'em.

I logged into my computer and went to our website to check our stats.

I just launched a new website, and was excited to see how it was doing. As I logged in, I was shocked to see my statistics. I lost $1,567 from the day before. This was after implementing all that you have learned so far in this book. Yet, we were still dealing with a losing offer. (You'll learn the last "secret" ingredient in this chapter, which wound up taking this campaign from loser to winner, which makes this chapter critical.) But back to the $1,567 loss…

Wow, I thought. That's horrible.

What would you do if you lost $1,567 in your first day with a new website? Would you pause everything you are doing, and say, "Well, I guess this won't work." Or would you say, "Great, we got a result; let's see how we can make this work."

The latter was my response. So I started focusing on how to make this work. The good news for me was this wasn't the first time I had lost money when starting a new website/business. It's part of the process of building a successful website or business in a new niche or market. We do all the work from the first 4 steps of Reverse Online Profits™ to set ourselves up for this most critical time. This is the time when we must decide and figure out if this new business or market is one we want to ramp up or decide it won't work, dump it, and move on to another idea.

The first few days of launching a business or website can be what make the difference between profit and loss.

For me, the initial results didn't look too exciting, as we took a decent loss. But, I was excited we had some traffic and a result to show for it. That's a success. In this chapter we will go into the process we use to decide whether to ramp it up or dump it.

I followed what you are about to learn, and within a few days, the losing campaign starting making us up to $2,000 a day! Frankly, I was amazed by the turnaround.

I've had many ideas that I thought were million-dollar ideas. I've pursued many of them, and some have cost me more than $1 million dollars in business. But, one thing I have become an expert at today is knowing when to fold 'em and when to hold 'em (taking a line from a famous Kenny Rogers song, "The Gambler").

The Success Principle

You gotta know when to hold 'em and know when to fold 'em.

I laugh at myself as I share this with you. I have been the poster child of the failure pitfall described above. Pride is an ugly thing. It's amazing how many people I have coached who are just like I was. They don't know when to fold 'em and move on. There is so much opportunity online, so for you or I to get stuck on one idea that keeps losing money is a waste of time. It costs us dearly in money, time, energy, and life.

For me, my worst "hold 'em" mistake was a software company I attempted to build for over three years. I invested close to $1 million dollars in that company. I had a stroke. I lost three years of my life to long working days, piled-up stress, and much more.

I had a large office with a lot of employees. I fell in love with the idea of building a large software company and then selling it for hundreds of millions of dollars in a few years. I knew what I wanted the software to do. The problem was executing that idea with the right team and the right timing . . . and it just wasn't going to be what I had envisioned.

I was traveling and promoting the software. I was getting thousands of clients, but the thing missing was our ability to deliver on the software I wanted to build. It just wasn't going to happen. I didn't have the experience to lead a team of software programmers nor did I have the cash flow to keep it going.

So my "good idea," which actually got results, was turning into a nightmare. And, this nightmare would have taken all I had if I had held on, but I finally made the decision to walk from that company and move in another direction.

It's never an easy place to be when you need to dump an idea, business, offer, or product. But once you break through and do it, you will find what I have discovered: in every instance, I immediately found an opportunity that made me more money in about half the time or less.

It hurts; it really does. But the reward for moving on is enormous.

When I finally "folded 'em" on the software company, another door of opportunity opened to me immediately.

It's amazing how that works in life. I learned years ago that I had to let go of certain things. Someone had me take a ball and put it in my right hand. He then asked me if I could catch another ball in my right hand without letting go of the ball that was already in my right hand. I said no. He explained to me that this is how life works. If you are holding on to something, you can't be ready for the new thing coming your way. Many times, you miss out on opportunities because your hands are too busy trying to hold on to something that you need to let go of.

Let me repeat that statement. It's critical. It will speak to you.

Many times, you miss out on opportunities because your hands (or heart) are too busy trying to hold on something that you need to let go of.

As soon as I let go of the software company, I started a new company, which has gone on to earn close to $20 million in a short period of time.

Figure out where you are in your business or with a product, service, or offer. The good news is it may be time to "hold 'em" and start ramping up your business. The other good news is it might be time to "fold" on the offer, service, or product. Either way, there is a bright future and profits to be made!

Let me address the Reverse Online Profits™ system's step 5 with one major, easy-to-do strategy to really start ramping up and banking on your business.

Ramp and Bank

Ramping up and banking is the difference between success and failure in most cases. Many times, people start a business online. They go out and make a few things happen.

They get a result. The result may be they didn't get any net profits in their first week or thirty days.

The next thing they do is quit. They say things like, "I don't know why this won't work."

Most people make a mistake when they confuse a loss as "failure" instead of "potential." I see initial losses as "potential." Granted, sometimes the losers will just be losers. But, the majority of the time, if we've done everything outlined in the first four steps of the Reverse Online Profits™ system correctly, we should be able to make any website or business profitable following the simple system.

In this crucial step 5 of the Reverse Online Profits™ system, we'll cover how to ramp and bank. Here's a recap of where you are in the process.

In this step, you'll learn that if most people would push a little harder and take a few more simple actions, they could take a losing business and turn it into a cash-producing powerhouse.

This step is all about ramp, bank, or dump.

This is basically the step where we find out if an advertisement or even a business is something we can:

- Ramp up to profitability; or

- Dump because it's a loser.

Being able to distinguish one from the other as fast as possible will save and make you a lot more money.

If you were able to show a result, meaning you made some money with the enterprise you started, then congratulations! Making that first dollar on a new business or campaign is often one of the hardest steps. It also sets you apart from most potentially successful business people on the planet. You took action and got a result. Now, let's see if that result can get better or if you need to dump the idea.

Make Money with Ads and Offers

Let's start with the steps you can take to make money with an advertisement and offer that is close to break-even. If your offer is not making you money, but not losing much either, there are a few steps you can take to turn a mediocre campaign into a winning one through my ramp and bank system.

1. Let your advertisement run for at least 24 hours on a limited budget (200 percent to 300 percent of what one sale will make you).

2. Review the Green Light System:
- Remember this system had four core lights and two of them had to be green for us to even be at the point where we are right now. Did the website you found:

- have high traffic? (Green Light No. 1)

- have consistent traffic? (Green Light No. 2)

- have traffic on multiple media sources? (Green Light No. 3)

- or could we recreate the offer? (Green Light No. 4)

- Think through these four Green Lights. How good do you feel about your current strategy? Was your idea green on Light No. 1 and Light No. 2? If not, then maybe you shouldn't be doing this business.

(NOTE: In coaching many people, I have found that this is the point where most people make a mistake. Even with the knowledge of Lights No. 1 and No. 2, most people—focused on what they think will work— skip through this system. That is a huge mistake. Let this system help reduce your chances of failure.)

3. Look at all the data you have collected from the current traffic to your website.

    a. Ask yourself: What could we improve? Some common questions are:
- Can we lower the cost for the advertisement?
- Could another ad do better?
- Can we get a higher click through on our ads?
- How can we make more from the traffic on our site?
- How can we pre-sell traffic better?
- Is our website communicating the same message as the advertisement?

4. Take these initial actions to make your idea profitable:

    a. Focus on reducing your costs for the advertising.

- If you are using PPC on search engines, use strategies to lower the cost per click from your ad.

- If you are using PPC on search engines, see if you can pause losing keywords (easy to track on most websites).

- If you are using Facebook.com, test and get ads to get more attention and clicks so your costs go down.

- If it's a media buy, negotiate to lower your cost for the ad.

- Analyze congruency of ads. Does the ad match the website?

    b. Focus on increasing your back end.

- Can you make more money with your list of people?

- Can you sell more products on the initial order?

- Can you increase the frequency of the buy?

- Can you increase the conversions on the people coming to your website?

- Can you get a higher commission or payout if you're promoting someone else's products?

These are the first actions you can take to make a website more profitable. There are some more in-depth strategies, but they will cover the top 80 percent of the actions you can take to get the best results.

You can get our more in-depth checklist at jeffusner.com/bookbonus.

If after testing all of the above, you are still not making money and can't make it work, consider another approach, offer, or idea.

A Pitfall to Avoid

Don't fall in love with your idea.

Always let the numbers guide your decisions, not your own emotions or pride.

The Most-Overlooked Ways to Double Your Business

In 2002, I was creating thousands of leads every month on the Internet for people looking for legal help. I did what I am teaching you in this book and was seriously cranking it.

I actually had more orders to fill than the leads I could create. I had a problem. If I could figure out a way to make more leads (get more traffic), I could instantly double my business.

I attempted to buy media in different areas, according to the strategy I've shared, and that worked, but I was still plateauing in our business. Our profits were flat.

I remember wondering about how I could get more traffic. What could I do? I sat looking at the search results on Google.com, pondering how to get more traffic. I saw all my competition listed above me and below me on different keywords.

I knew if I got to the No. 1 listing, I'd get more traffic, but then what? I had the No. 1 position on most of the keywords I really wanted. Then what?

Then it hit me. Why do I only have one ad on this keyword? I know it makes me money, so what if I launched another ad? How could I do that? It was easy; I just created another account and set up another website similar to the one that was working for me already. I advertised this new website in my new account. Instantly, I almost doubled my business and lead flow.

Wow, I thought. I wonder if I could do that again. And so I did. Eventually, on some keywords, I owned positions 1 to 5. I owned the first page.

I spoke of this earlier in the book. The interest is "real estate." When you find a money-making "block," you need to buy up the block! You can use this strategy in any media. Any website, search engine, Facebook, whatever.

The concept is simple.

Become Your Own Competitor

One of the best ways to ramp up a winning campaign or business is to simply become your own competitor.

This seems like a crazy strategy for most people, yet if you have ever been to an Olive Garden restaurant, you'll usually find another restaurant owned by its parent company—Darden—nearby, such as Red Lobster or Longhorn Steakhouse. Large corporations use this strategy and so should you.

I live in a small town and even here we have four McDonald's restaurants! Have you ever seen a Starbucks coffee shop right across the street from another of its own? I have, countless times.

Why would Starbucks do this? Place two of its coffee shops right across the street from each other. That's crazy, you might think.

Well, they are laughing their way to the bank, along with many other major corporations in America.

Owning more of the Internet real estate and competing against yourself is easy to do online. You can create another website and funnel traffic to it to sell your product, service, or information packaged in a different way.

This is an advanced strategy, but I've found this one strategy alone has helped increase our profits in some cases by up to 500 percent.

I think of any website as online real estate. If you find a website with traffic that makes you money or a search term that makes you money, you want to own all the real estate on the block.

Does this make sense?

You can do this, and when you do, you will wonder why you didn't do this in the past. It works in almost every business space. Don't just compete against your competitor — become your competitor and knock your competitor out of the space!

You will be amazed when you start to really dig deep and follow the ownership of large, well-known companies and brands. You wouldn't believe the number of companies that are actually owned by the same holding groups. Direct competitors owned by the same people.

Why? Because it works. Because it makes money.

You can and should do this in any market on the Internet. Dating, wedding planning, boat repair, weight loss, vitamins, real estate, retail, etc. Anything. Compete against yourself. Take up more of the market share.

Think about it. You already have the systems and processes in place to be successful. Why try to start something new, when you are not sure how you are going to do it? I'd rather focus my efforts in replicating myself to compete against myself. I can do this faster, and with more profits from the start.

Work Within Your Existing Business

It's always easier to ramp and bank on an existing business and channel than to create a brand-new one.

Take this point: I have seen countless successful people get bored with what they are doing, so they go out and invest their time and money in a brand-new business that has nothing to do with their current business or strategies.

The result: epic failure!

Why?

A new business takes a lot of energy and, oftentimes, requires different connections, different processes, different systems, and different websites to be successful.

Once you find something that makes money, focus at least 80 percent of your time scaling it up.

In your business, once you get to a point where you are successful and making money, always look to grow within your existing business model and system, and within your channel.

If you want to get into a new business, try to partner with someone who has the expertise that you don't have in the new industry, and you can bring what you do have to help make it a success. This is a much better strategy.

When ramping up your business, stay within your strengths. Don't get into something you don't know much about. Whether you are ramping up an offer, or ramping up your business, stick to what you know. Find new ways to market to your customers. Find new products they will buy. Focus on increasing revenues from what is making you the most money. This is the best way to ramp up any business.

And on that note, let's move to the next chapter, where I will share possibly the biggest lesson I learned, which ties right into staying within your strengths. In the next chapter, I'll share with you how I've learned to stay within my strengths and stay out of the technical side of building a business on the Internet.

I'm no techie, but the results we have created will shock you. Let me reveal to you another mistake I made—a $42,000-a-month mistake. Let's get to it.

CHAPTER 9
The Game Changer

In life, there are many moments when you look back and say, "That was a game-changing moment for me. My life will never be the same."

For me, one of these moments hit me when I made a mistake. To be exact, it was a $42,000-a-month mistake. Here's what happened.

For three years of my life, I had focused on building a software company. I sank endless amounts of dollars and hours into this company. I worked long days using every ounce of strength I had to make the company successful. The result: I failed miserably. In fact, I was bleeding up to $42,000 a month or more just from one mistake. And, I did this for close to two years. During this period, I almost died from a stroke due to all the stress. I was drowning in debt and becoming a father who never saw his wife or kids. This was the exact opposite of what I promised I would do. Yet, there I was.

I felt stuck. I had a staff of nearly twenty people in Colorado. I had a team of five to seven computer programmers in California working nonstop around the clock. Most nights, I would fall asleep between 3 a.m. and 4 a.m., often using my computer as a pillow. I would wake up a few hours later, my fingers still "attached" to my computer that was flashing with about fifteen instant messages received while I was sleeping.

Looking in from the outside, the company appeared to be doing fine. Sales were growing faster than we could keep up with. But from the inside, we were bleeding cash like a gunshot wound to the heart. I learned a huge lesson during this time.

High gross profits mean nothing. It's what you take home that matters.

Worse yet, if you are sacrificing your life for high gross profits and low net profits, you have created a situation where you have the lowest-paying job on the planet! In fact, for most of that time, I didn't draw any salary. I simply kept putting all the money we made (and a lot of my personal money) back into the company.

Then, the moment came when I found myself lying on the carpet at home weeping. I was overwhelmed, stressed, and desperate. I had given everything I had to build this company, and yet I wasn't sure how I would even afford food for my family. I had come to a point where enough was enough.

In that moment, I made a decision. A decision that would change my life forever. A decision to radically transform the face of my current business and future companies.

I decided to design my business around my lifestyle, instead of wrapping my lifestyle around my business. Here's what that means. I decided how I wanted to live and what I would be willing to sacrifice to build my business. I set boundaries that were not to be crossed in order to protect my life and my family.

I walked away from the philosophy I grew up with—where I had to work long, hard hours to make a good living.

I started to focus on what could I do if I were to commit to giving myself at least seven to ten weeks of vacation a year. To giving myself the option to live anywhere in the world. To not be cornered into working long hours to survive.

I stopped putting my main focus on business and began filling the gaps later with God, my wife, kids, time, and sanity. I began to put what was most important to me first in line. For years, I thought to myself, "I'll get through this phase of my business. The workload will surely lighten. Then, I'll get my life back. Then, I'll have time for ____, ____, ____ and ____."

What happened instead was the phase of: "I'll just make it through this part. Pushing harder and harder in life, doing whatever it takes." But this phase never stops unless you decide to stop it. There's always too much to do.

This chapter — and really this entire book — is about helping you succeed in your business and your life. But how do you do that? A large part of that answer is what I want to teach you next — how to automate and scale your company without having to sacrifice everything else in your life.

In fact, my goal is to go a step further. I want to show you how to be at least twice as effective with less than 50 percent of the hours you invest in your business currently.

Let's get into the process and systems I use now. These enable me to work fewer than 20 hours a week for many weeks, and to vacation anywhere in the world at will, while still growing several companies with increased profits.

Remember, I said leverage is a key to wealth. Well, here we are again. I believe you can create major leverage in your life.

Let me step back a moment. If you are just getting started online, this might be the most important chapter of this book. I know what it's like to want to get out from where you are. I know what it's like to dream about what could be. To dream about what your life will look like once your business is cranking. I also know what it's like to start a business at a time when you need to make money with your business or else you don't eat. I've been there.

The Right Way to Start

This chapter is going to teach you the right way to start . . . . From wherever you are right now to wherever it is you want to go. I'm excited you've made it to this part of the book. Even if you only implement a few strategies from this chapter, your life will never be the same. Whether you are building your first website or you have a successful website or business, this chapter can be a game changer for you.

This chapter will also show you how to take the five steps of Reverse Online Profits™ to create systems around you that scale your business by leveraging yourself through others (even if you are on a budget).

I've invested countless hours in exploring how to outsource as much of my work as I can while still scaling a business to massive profitability. When I was almost died, and then made some decisions to change my lifestyle, I cut almost 90 percent of my overhead in just a few weeks. And over the next year we had increased our revenues by almost 300 percent. My life was completely changed forever. Your life can change, too.

As we get into this area of leverage, the first thing you must do is to decide the parts of your business that you want someone else to help build. You could have an existing company and want to grow a new division. Or maybe you are launching a new business. You must make these decisions as quickly as possible so you can focus on what are the most important activities for your company to succeed.

Over the years, I've hired and fired close to a hundred people in my companies. These people were either from my own backyard or from the opposite side of the planet. Through these experiences, I've learned the best activities for which I need to hire workers, and the activities that I never want to hire for.

Make Hiring Decisions

Throughout all the different employees and outsourcers I have worked with, I've learned a few key questions to focus on when doing this successfully. Unfortunately, many of these questions came through me making mistakes, and then figuring them out. So my hope is you will use these questions now, before you make some of the mistakes I have made.

Whether you work all by yourself or have a large company, the process is the same. We are attempting to find your highest-leveraged activities and get you focused there. By simply doing this, your business could double within thirty to sixty days. Answer these four powerful questions:

1. What is the No. 1 activity I dislike doing but must be done for my company to grow?

2. What is the No. 1 activity I do but am not good at doing?

3. Where am I most effective with my company?

4. What do I enjoy doing the most?

For me, the answers to these questions haven't changed much since I started this activity. I still take time to get away from my normal routine to examine myself. Sometimes, this is just over a cup of coffee at a coffee shop, and other times, I get out of town, away from all the busyness in my life. Then, I take time to reflect. I have developed new skills along the way, but the answers are similar to those when I began. That's why the exercise works whether you are on day one in a business or thirty years into a business.

I have close to a hundred journals filled with notes, thoughts, strategies, and ideas from all the years I've invested into building businesses and building my life. When I go through questions like these, I take the time to write down the answers so that I can come back and read them tomorrow, a week from now, or a year from now. I can keep track of the answers to check if I am on course or not.

The No. 1 activity I dislike doing, but that has to be done, is anything technical on the Internet. This includes building websites, connecting websites to email programs, creating graphics, and dealing with servers and domains. Really, I dislike doing anything technical.

Asking myself the second question—regarding the No. 1 activity I do but am not good at doing—I realized I was getting stuck in the details of my business. I am not good at tracking every detail. I don't enjoy accounting. I don't like getting a ton of emails. I don't like having to manage the people doing all the details. I don't like customer service. I don't like gathering statistics on different marketing campaigns. I don't like working on something once it is started.

I like to get things moving, and then have other people help keep it moving.

Asking the third question, I found I am most effective in three main areas:

1. Doing market research (step 1 of the ROP system)

2. Creating offers and writing marketing copy

3. Visualizing and strategizing for the future

These are valuable areas in a company. I realized that if I could invest most of my time in these areas, I would be much more effective and make a lot more money.

For the fourth question, I had to say that I most enjoy planning strategies, systems, visions, funnels, and traffic growth.

These are also valuable skills for my companies. These activities could be worth a lot of money, so it's better to have me focused on them and not dealing with customers.

There are no right or wrong answers to these questions. The key is when I make my first hire, I am going to make sure the activities they do will be similar to my answers to questions No. 1 and No. 2.

If you did this activity and you hired one person, either locally or overseas, your business would increase (as long as you take the time you would have spent doing those activities you dislike or are not good at, and spend that time instead on the other activities to make your business money).

Another value of these questions is they keep you focused on figuring out ways to grow your companies and leverage your current assets without having to sacrifice your personal freedom.

Here's what's key to me: I want to work on projects/ companies that will not force me to go outside the limits I placed on my time.

For some of you, this doesn't apply. You love and want to work 80-hour weeks. I understand that. I've been there. For others, this chapter is going to be all about just getting other people to help you build your business, and doing it without costing you an arm or a leg. And for other readers, this chapter will give you the keys to freedom in your life.

It's the part where you will be able to effortlessly start and launch new companies and ideas on the Internet and do the work you love doing the most.

Work the Magic for You

The world we live in is changing. Nowadays, people don't follow the same pattern—go to college, graduate, get a job, work for the same company for forty years, and get a great retirement. This is a rarity. In fact, most people graduate college with a huge debt (the equivalent of a small mortgage) and fight to get a job that pays $20,000 to $30,000 a year. Plus, they have to compete against people on the other side of the globe who will do the same or better work for about 10 percent of that salary.

That's not good news if you are just getting out of college and are focused on the outdated plan above. But it is excellent news if you are ready to take your skills to a new level.

Today, you can hire people outside the United States—wonderful people—to work for you for as low as $1 to $2 an hour. These people will do an incredible job and be loyal to you for life. They will see this wage as a great wage and they will live a great life helping you build your company. As the U.S. economy has slowed, there are many countries in the world that are bursting at the seams with growth.

Overseas Hiring

One of the biggest game changers in your lifetime is the ability to hire people on the other side of the planet. You can talk with them on Skype as if they are next door. You can manage them just as easily as your employees sitting right beside you. And you don't have to deal with all the issues of having employees (drama, salaries, taxes, laws against business owners). All this — at about 90 percent less money than before.

This opens the door to anyone on a budget to start leveraging themselves through other people. In the past, most people couldn't afford hiring someone to work for them. Training new people not only takes a lot of time, but you have to learn new laws about having employees, pay more taxes, and have less time to focus on your business.

Today, when you have an opportunity to hire someone full time for around $200 a month, it means that almost anyone in the United States can hire a worker. Think about that for a second. For most people, that amounts to a cell phone bill or a cable bill. If they'd just cut their cable or cell phone service off, they would have plenty of money to build a large company. That's sounds pretty ridiculous, doesn't it? But it's true!

When I took action on this idea, I cut about $42,000 a month in overhead and increased my profits by hundreds, even thousands of percentage points within four to six months. This is a game changer. It's life changing.

You can get this kind of help in almost any area: bookkeeping, building websites, writing sales copy, customer support, appointment setting, sales calls, billing, editing video, writing articles, writing a book, sending email, doing administrative tasks, building back links, posting to blogs and forums, setting up ads on Google, Yahoo, Facebook or other sites, building apps, doing research . . . and on and on and on.

In the past, these jobs would have taken a lot of time and money to do. In fact, most people would never have thought they could afford help with these jobs.

This is not the truth anymore.

You could have a full-time web designer working for you for less than $200 a month! Or you could hire people for almost any of these activities, or many together, for less than $200 a month.

Get this: when you can hire out work for close to $1 to $2 an hour, it frees you up to focus on the main activities in your business that:

- you love to do; and

- make you money.

This in turn frees up your life, gets rid of crazy stress, saves you money, and makes you money.

Guess what happens when you can save hundreds to tens of thousands of dollars each month? It's a beautiful thing. It's one of the keys to your success.

When you save this much money, you now have higher margins in your business. Higher margins mean you can mess up, fail, totally blow a ton of ideas, and still end up making money.

Seriously. This is amazing. When you can keep more money in your pocket by increasing your margins, you will have the opportunity to mess up a whole lot more!

To me, this is great news, because I take a lot of action, and a lot of times, it doesn't work out well. But I can do that now, because I use this strategy. And when the ideas do work, I can scale them faster than ever before for maximum leverage and profits.

One other magical, cash-producing activity begins with your business:

You can start working "on" your business versus "in" your business.

There is a major difference. When you work in your business, it is very stressful, slow moving, cash-sucking, and ineffective. When you work on your business, it is very low stress, high leverage, cash producing, and profitable.

There has never been a time to create leverage for yourself through other people than right now!

Work on Your Business Without Actually Working

At this point, I have to ask you something important, something big.

Would you like to have a way to get people working on your business for only $1 to $2 an hour? Or, the bigger question is how many people would you like to have working on your business for only $1 to $2 an hour?

Outsourcing Options

There are two ways that you can go about outsourcing the work:

- On a project basis

- On a full-time basis

When you outsource on a project basis, you hire someone to work on one project. When they are done with the project, that's it. You may never hear from them again. I've used this method of outsourcing to build many websites, many types of software, and other areas of my business.

There is a time and a place for outsourcing on a project basis. Here are some circumstances to use this method:

- When you can't figure out how you could keep a full-time person busy

- When you only want to get something done for your business one time and never again

Let me shed some light on the first reason above. Even if you can't keep a full-time person busy for 40+ hours a week, in most cases, it's still going to be cheaper to have a full-time person sitting around twiddling their thumbs at a low wage, than hiring someone part-time in the U.S.

Or, you could find one other person to partner with on a part-time basis. That way, you only pay $50 to $100 a month or so for someone working 20 hours a week on your business.

The second reason is valid. We've done this before and still do.

Where to Look

Here are two websites where we've found people to work on a project basis:

- Fiverr.com

- Elance.com

We have used other websites as well, so be sure to check the book bonus area of JeffUsner.com™ for the latest updates.

With fiverr.com, you simply do a search on the type of work you want done. Then you sort by the "highest rating" to see people who have a track record with great feedback. Don't expect the greatest work on Fiverr.com, because everything only costs $5. That being said, you can still get $5 worth of work and a whole lot more from someone on Fiverr.com.

Again, think of anything you need help with, especially on the tech side of your business, and Fiverr.com is a great way to go.

With elance.com, you will pay more money and generally get a better result. When working on a project basis, I like to have two or three different providers competing for our business. Many times, you can say, "We are looking for long-term help [say it only if it's true] and we want to see how you would handle _____." Fill in the blank. This could be something like, "coming up with a specific strategy to rank on the first page of Google for the term 'boat repair.'" This is an example for SEO (Search Engine Optimization). You want to see what they would say. You'll find out from their response if they know what they are doing, and you can learn more tricks about certain things you want done. Of course, you don't want to take advantage of people who you might not hire, so this approach is best used as a way to determine who might be the strongest hire(s) to add to your team.

The second way to outsource is to do it on a full-time basis.

I love this option, mainly because I've had some bad experiences when trying to work with companies on a contract basis, where we are one of their many clients. If you are just one of many clients, you will not get the attention and dedication you need to grow your company. Most companies or individuals you hire are trying to juggle your projects with those of several other clients. You are just a number, not their main priority. Their main priority is their own bottom line. What I've found is the "squeaky wheel gets the grease." If you don't stay on top of these people every day, your work will not get done.

Don't get me wrong on this. If you simply outsource by project, it is not like they cannot do a great job, but your project is just one of many fighting for attention.

There is a time and place to outsource by project, and I'll cover that in a moment.

If you hire someone or some people or a company solely focused on making your business successful, that is another story . . . a winning story in fact!

Think about it this way. Who do you think will accomplish more for your business: Ten people who work on your project while also working on ten projects for other clients, or five people fully focused on your business and tasks?

It's pretty obvious, right? You want a team who will work for you on your projects alone, because it is all about focus.

My Experience with Outsourcing

We started hiring good people from the Philippines a few years ago. We started with one person and grew from there. Now we have a team of about ten people based in the Philippines. The best part is they are getting great results for us, and our payroll is cut by about 90 percent!

Here's how I started to write this book. We have a writer who works full time for us writing articles, blog posts, ebooks, etc. To write this book, I asked her to watch some videos of me speaking about the Reverse Online Profits™ System and then transcribe the videos. Within about five days, she sent almost 27,000 words for the book. The book was about 300 words per page, so I had about 90 pages of this book written for less than $100. This got the book project moving fast, and the investment was minimal.

All the websites we build now are done by our team in

the Philippines. We've created about a hundred new websites in the last year, all created overseas. And our cost is next to nothing. We have some incredible graphics people who create most of the graphics we use in our business, from book covers to website images to brochures. We've built custom software for our business to automate processes and make money, all done by people who are focused 100 percent on making our company grow.

India vs. the Philippines

I started hiring workers in India in 2003 or 2004. I still have one employee from back then building out software for our company. Hiring in India can be a bit more of a challenge. When I first began working with people in India, it was stressful, because we had major communication issues. I would type one thing I wanted to have done, and when I saw what was done, it didn't look close to what I had asked for. The worker didn't understand my communication for what I wanted. He could not understand what I was talking about through instant messaging. (This was before Skype and the project management we do today.)

I spent many late nights working at 3 a.m., because it's about a 12-hour difference in time zones, trying to get websites and software built. There were mornings my wife would wake up early and see me still sitting there hours later pulling my hair out, because my programmer in India didn't understand what I was communicating to him.

I fought through those communication gaps, and now I am able to get a lot more done with him. He has learned more about what my company needs and how we think.

But it's a totally different story with people from the Philippines. Many of them speak American English so well that you'd think you were talking with someone from down the street. In fact, many of them speak English better than I do. Unlike Indians, the Filipinos speak English as their first language.

If you visit their country, you will find that everyone speaks American English, from the cab drivers to utility personnel to fishermen.

Communication Is the Lifeblood

Right now, we only hire workers in the Philippines versus India, because we've had some great success there. I love the people, their talents and skills, and I love the easy communication. If you hire four people from the United States to do routine tasks for your business, you might have a payroll of about $16,000 a month. But, if you outsource the work over to the Philippines, you get the same high quality of work from four people for as little $800 a month. Can you imagine how huge your savings would be? Again, this allows you to have much higher profit margins.

It is totally worth it. You'd also be surprised to know that the Filipinos who do this work all have college degrees! It's really awesome, and you can use this pool of talent to grow your business and reach your full potential.

The killer part is that Filipinos are not spoiled brats who approach the world like they are entitled to something. They do not give you minimal work just to get by so that you don't fire them. They honor you and your business.

8 Tips to Successful Outsourcing

Outsourcing sounds almost too good to be true. So how do you it? And what is the best way to do to? Well, the good news is it really is this good. The bad news is that it does take some work to build a team. I say bad news, because this isn't just some fantasy. It's like any team you would build to grow a business. But do not worry, because the benefits of getting outsourcing overseas are massive.

1. Be patient with yourself and others. It is all anchored in patience. First you have to start looking for people online and interviewing them. Not everybody is born with killer skills so you have get out there, be patient, and give people a chance. Think of your outsourcing as an investment. You have to grow it and stick with it, but once it takes flight, it's going to take you where you've never been before.

2. Don't expect instant returns. People need time to be trained and to learn about your business. Give them time. This is where your initial investment comes in. Don't think of what it costs to hire and keep these people, but think of what it costs not to have them around. Don't expect huge returns right away, because they will come eventually. Celebrate small victories in the beginning. Be a good finder and encourage anything positive that you see.

3. Hire one person at a time. There is wisdom in not hiring a ton of people at once. It is better to start with one and get all the training done for this one person. Then, build from there. You do not want to experience the chaos of trying to run a huge team overnight. It will only stress you out and cost you money. Better to start slow; then eventually train someone to manage your team to free your time and leverage yourself even further.

4. Communicate. One of the most important keys to out-sourcing is communication. I have talked about my experience with communicating with my guy in India and the challenges I had there. To really make this work, you have to set up good communication. Usually what I do is provide instructions on what I want done, maybe show an example or two, and then usually my people would get it done the next day. You just have to talk it out and things fall into place.

It is worth investing considerable time into communicating your project parameters and expectations upfront before starting a new project or working with a new outsourcer. You must be clear on what you want. Showing examples of what you want will go a long way. We use software called Basecamp. You can check out the book bonus section at JeffUsner.com™ to see how to get started with this web-based project management tool. It makes communicating with my team on the other side of the globe almost flawless. We are so much more productive because of this tool.

Another tactic I use with my overseas team and the people in our office in Texas is to ask for a report on daily tasks. Here's how this works. At the end of every day, each person posts about his/her work and experiences on our communication board (easy to do). Here's what I or the person who is managing the particular person want to know:

*   What are your top priorities for tomorrow?
*   What did you accomplish today?

- What challenges did you run into?

- Do you need my help/advice with anything you experienced today? If so, what do you need?

This way, I now know their top priorities for the next day, and I can adjust if necessary. I know what they got done today and what I or someone on my team can do to help them get better or move faster on their priorities.

It's a simple system you should use in your business and with your team.

5. Treat your people like people, because they are! When your people do good work, give them a bonus. Reward them. Encourage them. Find out more about them, the things they love, and what do they like to do. Then try to reward them in those areas. Also, be aware of their local customs and holidays. For example, the week of Easter is a holy week in the Philippines and most Filipinos expect to take off several days during this week. We granted this time off because it is their custom, and it honors and respects their traditions.

6. Get your legal documents in order. As with any person doing work with your company, be sure to have non-disclosure agreements and other documents signed to protect your work and intellectual property.

7. Set clear expectations and project milestones. You need to measure progress. What is getting done? Are we on schedule? If it's taking longer, why? Again, this

goes back to communication, but you need to make sure there are deadlines and goals for progress. Then, you need to stick to them and have consequences if there are issues.

8. Record everything. When you are training someone on a task, always record it. You can use Jing or Camtasia software from Techsmith.com. The key to ensuring your business succeeds as it grows is to enable it to replace you. The goal is to have your business generating revenue, even when you are not working in it.

   Whatever tasks you are doing every day, write a description of it. Ask yourself what you could teach someone else to do. At first, this may feel weird, but after you achieve a breakthrough and do it, you'll want to repeat the process with everything!

   Record everything so you can train people in your office or on the other side of the world in the same way.

Outsource Everything but the Kitchen Sink

There is no limit to what you can and cannot outsource. We have even outsourced some of our legal stuff using lawyers on elance.com. It is not the big legal stuff but the small legal stuff that saves you a couple thousand dollars.

In general, you want to outsource your low-paying activities so you can focus on the highest paid activities. This way, you are not bogged down on the low-productivity tasks, and you can focus on the high-leverage tasks.

Remember how we talked about focus and the importance of identifying your top activities for you to do?

For example, if your goal is to personally make $100 an hour, I would definitely outsource the tasks that cost about $2 an hour, because your time is worth more. This action alone saves you about $98 every hour. Instead of doing the activity that you don't like and aren't good at, you could outsource it and use the time to find ideas for a new business or come upon a new idea to make money, which will return to you more than the $2 per hour you spend outsourcing tasks that simply take more time without generating more revenue for you.

Successful Formula for New Outsourcing

We follow three simple rules when hiring a new outsourcer:

1. **Make the first project a challenge.** Don't give them easy tasks to start. You want to see how well they accomplish the challenge. Again, it's important to communicate with them. With many Filipinos, when they don't know something, they go silent. Make sure your outsourcers know from the beginning to be open in their communication with you and to bring any issues or challenges they have to you.

    Their first task is important. If they don't do a good a job on this, they probably won't improve. It's no different than hiring someone in your own office where you can watch over them every day. If someone doesn't do their best to impress you in their first week at work, fire them. Working with that person will only get worse. Working with outsourcers is no different. Find out what you have right away. Then, either keep them working for you or let them go, and find someone else who will do a better job.

2. **Give them good specifications of projects.** I mentioned this earlier, but it's worth repeating this point. I've had projects that took three to five times as long as they should have, because I didn't invest enough time upfront in making sure that I was clear about the needs of the project. Take time to outline every detail, give good examples, and then go back over it again with them. It will be worth it. Once you give them the specifications, set proper expectations and goals for completion.

3. **Watch the results.** I always focus on results. People can talk the talk. They can say they will do this or that. But, the bottom line is: What are their results? What did they get done? Did I get excuses or did they do what we agreed to, according to step 2? It's pretty straightforward, so watch what they do. In my experience, most projects will take about twice as long and cost twice as much as initially planned, regardless of how well you spec out a project and set deadlines. This is just the reality of building businesses online. But don't let your people know that you understand projects can take twice as long to complete. However, don't be surprised and mad when people don't hit deadlines. Extend some grace and reevaluate deadlines. Come to new agreements and move forward.

The Hiring Process

We use several websites to find talent online. I suggest you to go to the book bonus section at JeffUsner.com™ to see the resources we are using for hiring.

Let's walk through our hiring process:

1. Using the websites we suggest at JeffUsner.com™, do a search for the skill or talent you are looking to hire.

2. Email the people you think have potential. Here's what our emails look like when we hire:

[Email subject]

Job Position with American Company

[Body of email]

Hi, we have a full-time position available for you in an American company. We are contacting you to see if you have in interest in working part time or full time with us. The position would require [insert the job description] and the pay would be [insert the salary up for grabs]. Please let us know if you have an interest in this position. Please include examples of your work with [insert the particular task or skill] when you reply.

Regards,

Jeff Usner

3. Always contact the people with the most recent resumes (one week or less). Work with the freshest people looking for work. You'll have much better results.

4. Send out about ten to fifteen emails to people you might want to work with, using the example from point No. 2.

5. You'll usually hear back from four to six people.

6. You'll hire one or two people after exchanging some emails and reviewing their work.

7. One of these people sticks with you.

A tip on step No. 2 above: If you don't know what description to use for the part that says what we are looking for/require, simply look at what others are doing on the same website. Or go to craigslist.com in San Francisco (or another tech city) if you are hiring a tech position, and do a search there as a job hunter to see the results. Read through them, find one you like, copy and paste and modify to fit your needs. Then use it. (Hint: This is how I post on Craigslist as well. If you are modeling your job description on one from a different city, the process works great.)

You will be shocked by the talent pool you can hire. You will love this!

One other gold nugget for you:

Have you heard of the website Fiverr.com? On this website, you can basically get almost anything done for five dollars. Now, not all, but a lot of the tasks that used to take you hours or someone else hours to do can be done on Fiverr. com. This is a great website to hire someone on a project basis, as you have very little money to risk and you have major potential for incredible results.

In fact, you may find people who do excellent work, who you might hire full time in the future!

Here's what we've found is the best way to use Fiverr. com: Let's say we are doing some SEO (search engine optimization) on our website. When we do this, we may shoot a video to distribute on Youtube.com with links back to our website.

This can be an effective strategy to build links into your site for SEO. (SEO isn't a topic for this book. But, be sure to look at JeffUsner.com/bookbonus for some exciting ways we can help you with your SEO.)

There is a tool called "Traffic Geyser" that will push your video out to hundreds of websites on the Internet, creating a lot of links back to your website. This can create a considerable amount of free traffic for your website.

In the past, we paid hundreds of dollars every month to use the Traffic Geyser software. Now all we do is go to Fiverr.com and do a search for "traffic geyser video submission," and we will find many people who will do this for us for only five dollars. We save the money by not having to pay for the software, and we don't have to spend all the time doing the activity ourselves. We just give the person on Fiverr.com our link/video and they go to work. All for five dollars.

A keypoint when hiring on Fiverr.com: When you do a search for a topic, like "traffic geyser video submission," you will see a lot of results. What you want to do is sort the results by clicking where it says "Sort gigs by." Then click on the word "rating."

This will give you the people with the best track record. Then simply click to hire them.

You can use Fiverr.com for all types of work. For example, graphics work, gifts to people, video, social marketing, writing, advertising, advice, website creation, fan page timeline creation, and much, much more.

Fiverr.com has become one of our favorite websites to use. Please be sure to check at JeffUsner.com/bookbonus to see the latest websites we use to hire work on a full-time basis or on a project basis.

There you go. Simple enough, right? Figure out the best position to hire first, and then get to it.

Now that you know how to hire for pennies on the dollar for almost any job necessary to grow your business online with the Reverse Online Profits™ system, let's talk about your first steps of action. Without action, this book is useless to you. Action on ideas is what will change the face of your business. Let's put the excuses aside, and focus on what you can do and how you can do it now! Let's get your business rocking.

CHAPTER 10

Close, Call To Action, Bigger Visions

So what's next? Where do you go from here? I've given you all I can possibly fit into this book on how to succeed with an online business — and maybe even life. I've done my best to lay out the exact blueprint I've used to generate millions of dollars on the Internet. You have learned the exact system we use in our office every day to build several successful companies and help many others grow.

Let's review the Reverse Online Profits™ System one more time. Then, we'll discuss the best way to take action so you can get from wherever you are to wherever you want to be.

You now have a deep understanding of the simple five-step Reverse Online Profits™ system.

Here's a brief overview of the steps you learned:

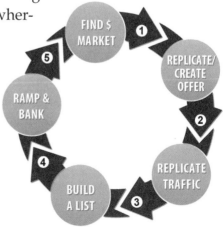

- Find a money website or market

- Recreate the offer

- Replicate traffic

- Build a list

- Ramp and bank

You've also learned how you can use this system whether you are a brand-new person starting a business or a successful businessperson who is focused on growing an existing business. This system works in any business, in any market, and at any time. And the great part is that you've also learned how you can outsource and hire people who will be able to do most of this work for you so you can actually have a life while building your business. Freedom and lifestyle are major goals for most of us, and this system will allow you to create the business you've dreamt of with the lifestyle to match it!

After reading this book, you will know more than 95 percent of the formula that anyone uses to market profitably on the Internet. You are set up for success. What you do now is what will determine your success or failure. What you do now will determine where you will be one month, one year, and five years from now.

Your life can look as different as mine does. From over $285,000 in debt, struggling, stressed out, almost dying from a stroke, not knowing what to do on the Internet, and trying everything with nothing to show for it . . . to being featured on ABC's Secret Millionaire show as one of the top Internet marketers in the world!

And all this happened in a little over two years!

I am amazed by my own story every time I hear it. Many times, I sit and just look in the mirror and think, "Wow, how did this happen?" I literally spent about a year in shock at what happened to us. And now, I'm focused on giving back and helping as many business owners as I can to take their businesses to the next level on the Internet.

It's your time. This book has enough strategies, techniques, and information to transform your life.

Don't Evaluate, Take Action

Some of you might be overwhelmed by all that you've learned in this book. Here are a few action steps for you.

1. Go to JeffUsner.com/thefinalchapter, where I've got a free gift for you. Because you made it this far into the book, I'd like to reward you. I'm proud of you. I'm honored and humbled that you listened to me through this book.

2. Decide on one idea you are going to take action on within the next twenty-four hours. Write it down, commit to it, and get it into action.

   Don't get locked into information overload. I would like you to go out and make a mess! Go out and get something moving.

3. Focus on your first dollar. If you are launching a new business, focus on the first dollar you can make.

   If you are applying these techniques to an existing

business, focus on generating your first dollar with these strategies.

Start with a small goal, get the result, and create momentum. Don't have a large idea that you never take action on. Get something laser-focused that can give you a result fast.

4. Start right where you are. If you are confused about what one idea to take action on or how to make your first dollar, I want you to look at what is right in front of you. Everything you need to get going is right in front of you. It may not be the "perfect" circumstances, or the "perfect" economy. That doesn't matter. Stop right now, and write down all the good things you have in front of you. Maybe you have a ton of ideas or possibilities, or maybe you have just one. Whatever the case, get focused on one thing right in front of you right now to take action on.

Once you see you can do this, your belief system will continue to increase, and you will get more and more done.

Many times we tend to overcomplicate things. We get overwhelmed about how to change our lives and about what to do next. We focus on a big vision, and we get stuck there.

We fantasize about what life will be like when our vision comes to pass. We find activities to keep us busy, without really ever getting productive. I don't know about you, but I like to complicate things. And that's so stupid of me. I am really only good at doing very simple things.

I'm a simple guy. Simple actions work best for me. So when you don't know where to start or you are looking for the best place to start, look at what is right in front of you.

Do it right now.

Start there.

If you apply all you that have learned, you will see your business grow. You will make more money. You will begin to create the lifestyle you desire. I know this. I hope you are starting to realize this fact. But, I'd also like to encourage you, as you continue to break through new financial barriers, to give back to those around you. Making a lot of money, growing companies, influencing those around you — all these are great — but after it's all said and done, if you haven't given back to others, you will feel empty. I've been there. So I want to encourage you to give back as you grow. Give back from where you are right now. Don't wait.

Give Back As You Grow

As you grow, ask yourself, "What are you giving with what you have?"

You may say, "Hey Jeff, that's easy for you to say, because you're a multimillionaire already."

Well, yeah, but if I had actually learned – and practiced this – earlier in my business, I might have become a multimillionaire sooner. So I'm trying to give you a shortcut to riches. If you can start giving back, starting exactly where you are, you will achieve all the money, fame, success, and joy you seek much more quickly.

I know, right now, you don't have enough time, money, energy, or resources to give more than you have now. You might still be struggling to feed your family, like I was. I understand; I've been there. But if I could share one piece of advice to the person I was when I was on that floor on my knees, in breakdown, it would be this: start where you are and give what you can in order to provide others with what they want. You will be rewarded with what you want.

In fact, that is what happened. I realized I had to start giving back right where I was. When I was desperate, I was living on cheap noodles every day, but that's the time I started to give back. When I had the least is when I formed the habit to give.

As I started to give back from the money I earned, I found that my income accelerated. Now, it's part of my business practice to give 10% of my gross revenue. With our businesses, when money comes in the door, we immediately take 10 percent off the top and give it away. You might be thinking, "I can't give 10 percent; I am not even able to live off the 100 percent I have now." But, I challenge you to start where you are.

As you move forward using the systems in this book, as your businesses grow, as you create the lifestyle you desire, continue to ask yourself, "What am I giving back with what I have?"

On ABC's *Secret Millionaire,* I was so blessed to be involved with three incredible organizations, which are truly making a difference in many people's lives.

I was able to give back in a financial way to these organizations at the end of my week, but I was also able to make an impact earlier in the week when I was simply volunteering my time.

In fact, I went to a party for the organization Teamability. Here's something you may not know. I spent time with a young man named Orlando. He's an incredible example to all of us to become more and give back. When I was filming the show, everyone I met (including Orlando and his family) had no idea we filmed an episode for Secret Millionaire. So when I saw them a few months later at this party, they still didn't know what was about to happen and how the show would forever impact their lives.

When I saw Orlando's family members again months after we filmed the show, they immediately ran and gave me a huge hug and kiss, thanking me for the time I spent with their son Orlando. They had no idea I gave money to Teamability or about ABC's Secret Millionaire. Giving your time makes a bigger impact than you could ever imagine.

I realized on Secret Millionaire that, for my entire life, I had made excuses for why I couldn't volunteer, why I couldn't invest time in my local area. I was too busy with my life, with my wife, my kids, my companies, my friends, my family, and my employees with all the activities we have. But the reality is we all have time to give back to the communities that contribute to us — and in this case, this was the organization I chose to give to.

Giving of your time will change your life forever. You will never be the same. Ever.

A Little Goes a Long Way

On our recent trip to India, we took our sons Joel and Joshua with us. We had an amazing time giving back to the local communities and churches, helping business and community leaders. While we were in India, we visited an orphanage we love and support. My sons were able to see how these amazing kids live each and every day. They were able to see and help in any way they could. They learn everyday about the importance of giving back. (In fact, if you ask them what they do with their money they earn, they would tell you 'first we give to the orphans and the poor'.)

You would be shocked how the smallest gifts have the biggest impact. One of the most incredible moments of our time at the orphanage was our last night there. We had brought a gift from the United States.

Some friends of ours have a toy business. They have tons of matchbox cars that they haven't been able to sell. So my wife told them we were going to be with 237 amazing boys in India. Without flinching, they offered close to 250 match-box cars to take with us for these boys.

At the end of our last night at the orphanage, we surprised the boys with this present. So far, I had not seen a toy there. Money is tight, so all the money the orphanage receives goes directly to feeding and clothing the boys. And here we were with these small matchbox cars. This present didn't cost hundreds or thousands of dollars — they were simply toys stored at someone's business. And now, they were going to be the best present these boys had ever seen.

As each boy came up to the box to pick out a toy, he shook our hands, looked us in the eyes with excitement, and said thank you. It was an amazing experience for all of us. But, it was especially impactful to my sons Joshua and Joel, who stood by the box watching the enthusiasm on each boy's smiling face.

Giving back. This gift wasn't even from us. The people who gave these toys will be blessed. What do you have lying around your house that would make a difference in someone's life?

Do you have old toys? Clothes? Food? Furniture? What's stashed in storage that is taking up space? If you don't know where to start giving back, start with this: go unpack some boxes and give the items to needy families. I did this exercise back when I had no money. It was a good way for me to give back at that time.

If you don't know who needs help in your community, ask around. It won't take long to find people who are hurting. There are people hurting everywhere. We all hurt at some point in our lives. You may be hurting now, but you can still give back.

Giving back gives you vision. Giving back gives you purpose. Giving back gives you a mission. Giving back is the best thing you can do to help yourself in any situation. You can selflessly give back as much as you want. The people you help will be impacted, and you will probably be impacted even more.

Purpose of this Book

When I give of my time or money, I am the one who benefits the most. The purpose of writing this book is to encourage, inspire, motivate, and move you to do more, become more, and have more. Yet, as I write these words, as I invest countless hours into writing this book, I know I am benefiting the most.

Writing this book has helped me to clarify what motivates and inspires me. It has forced me to look deeper into myself than at any other time in my life.

That's how it works when I teach a group of people. I need to invest a lot of time preparing and honing my skills to teach a subject. When I do this, it makes me better at what I do. It makes me better with my vision, my excuses, my decisions, my pride, my skill sets, my comfort zones, my war on debt, my focus, my giving, and my actions. I can't help, but improve on these skills when I am teaching them. The teacher always seems to benefit more than the students. The teacher must be on the top of his/her game to effectively communicate with students in order to increase their skill sets and knowledge.

It's amazing.

I'd like to encourage you to take all the ideas you have learned in this book and go take action. That's the best reward I could receive. I'd love to hear from you. I would love to hear about how your life has changed.

Put this material into action. I believe this book is filled with more money-making content than any book I've ever bought myself. I believe there is more information in this book than what was in the $2,000 courses I've invested into in the past.

So, what's your excuse?

I don't think you or I have one. Let's go out there and change the world. Dominate your marketplace, and then give back.

May God bless you abundantly in every area of your life.